IRON *sharpens* IRON

IRON *sharpens* IRON

ERRICK A. FORD

Wisdom of the Ages

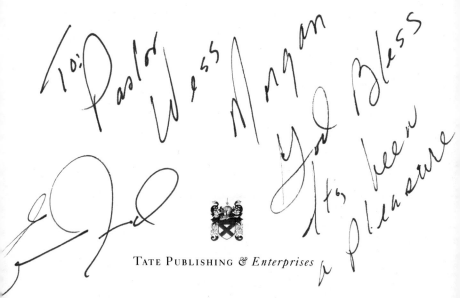

TATE PUBLISHING & *Enterprises*

Published by Tate Publishing & Enterprises, LLC
127 E. Trade Center Terrace | Mustang, Oklahoma 73064 USA
1.888.361.9473 | www.tatepublishing.com

Tate Publishing is committed to excellence in the publishing industry. The company reflects the philosophy established by the founders, based on Psalm 68:11,
"The Lord gave the word and great was the company of those who published it."

Book design copyright © 2010 by Tate Publishing, LLC. All rights reserved.
Cover design by Amber Gulilat
Interior design by Stephanie Woloszyn

Published in the United States of America

ISBN: 978-1-61566-793-2
1. Religion / Christianity / Amish   2. Philosophy / General
10.02.05

acknowledgements

I could not have accomplished this book without the help of the most precious people in my life. My father Willie Ford and my Mother Rosie Ford. My children Erica, Destini, and Errick (EJ). They have unconditional love for me. Special thanks to Stanley and Dionne Ford who have supported me continually on all my endeavors without fail.

Thank you all!
—*Errick A Ford*

CONTENTS

foreword

You don't have to say a lot to say something. I have always been intrigued by the words and advice of the people of the world. I have found that everyone had something to say and share. Even our youth are advising each other, good or bad in one way or another. We do it on the job, at school, and in everyday life. Its funny for instance, how that your son or daughter will not always listen to you, but they will listen to their friends. Even wives and husbands will not always listen to each other, but will listen and pay attention to what their friends have to advise. Books seem to rule. People will pick up a book, read it and apply it to their lives. For some odd reason books validate or invalidate the feelings or actions of the reader. We all would like to hear good advice from some of the best minds in the world. We all would also like to hear from the most educated among us. But what about mom and what about dad? Didn't they give us the most immediate advice? Didn't they make a very real impact on us? Were their words less effective than anything that we have read in books? People have different experiences and are able to learn and teach according to what they have been through. The teacher is really in all of us. The great names of our past are no better at sharing life's insight than our family and friends, but know this, they are drawing from areas of learning and experiences that can only be imagined. I thought it would be great to be able to bring so much of this diverse kind of wisdom and knowledge together into one book. One aspect of this book is the Alpha and Omega part. God has so much to say to us, but we are not always listening. I believe that he uses others to communicate to us the rights and the wrongs of the world that we live in. It doesn't matter if the person is spiritual or not, God can use whosoever he will to lead and to guide us. A bad man can give good advice, simply because you probably wouldn't have listened to anyone else. He is helping us along life's road whether we want to believe it or not. The large variety of people used gives you a broad perspective into the mind of some of the most historic figures. What they have to say applies to everyone. They are people like you and me, and some of the things they said holds true today. It is exciting to experience how profound some of the simplest things are. Beginning from 600 b.c. until today I have found that there is not much difference in thinking. Most and best of all is that not everything is in this book, but I made sure that everything that is in this book is something that you can use. This book gets to the point, short, sweet, to the point, you need it, and I need it.

introduction

IRON SHARPENS IRON
WISDOM OF THE AGES

Iron sharpens iron: close contact friction to knock off rough edges. All people develop rough edges naturally. We as people tend to try to help smooth out these same rough edges through everyday contact. We do this in the form of advice, wisdom, and/or counsel. This book has been written with the inspiration of helping others. When we say things that make sense, we appeal to people's sense of reason, and the listener is made better.

I was once young and now I am older, and I only have a few words of advice for the world. It took too long to gain some of the wisdom that I have now. This book is for the youth, the high schooler, the college student, and the adult. You don't have to lean on the limited advice handed down thus far in your life. Take some advice from the greatest, the brightest, and the most sincere ordinary people. "If there is a book that you need to read, but it hasn't been written yet, you must write it." This is a book that I read over and over, especially in times that I need something to inspire or encourage me. I use the knowledge that is given to settle me and comfort me. Knowing that there are so many that have gone before me and have the vision and understanding from so many points of view. I welcome what they have to say because they are speaking to the world and me.

God has so much to say to man, but man is not always listening, so he uses people to help us. The inspiring words of this book are particularly chosen, not lengthy, easy to read and understand. Allow the words to resonate and help you with how you think and feel about life. Apply this wisdom to your own life. "Wisdom of the Ages" is just that. Nothing noted in this book is without value to man. You will find that it is not only a book, but also a resource for and from all walks of life. I researched, listened, and I inquired. Nearly everyday I cataloged words of wisdom, and golden nuggets of wisdom that I could put in a book.

I believe that nearly everyone has something profound to say at some point in his or her life. Some quotes are from people's own experience, and some from the knowledge and experiences of others. That which comes out of the abundance of a man's heart is never ending, because "out of the abundance of the heart the mouth speaks" (Matt. 12:34). A hundred books could be written from the words of everyday man past and present. Each pearl of wisdom would be just as profound as the next. Because life, no matter how long or how short, brings about lessons learned, no matter how small.

Remember, "As iron sharpens iron, so a friend sharpens a friend" (Prov. 27:17).

"Everyone needs a book that they can open to any page, at any time and begin reading. Just start anywhere; the value is there" *(Errick A. Ford). (EAF)*

You will find that the Alpha and Omega is in the beginning, and He is at the end of this book.

His words are bigger and His name is bigger than all of the others in this book.

He has inspired man to think, say, and advise. Because "All things were made by Him; and without **Him** there was not anything made that was made." He is *"I Am"* and all entries were with respect to Him in mind.

you ... your ... he ...
him ... her ...

ALPHA

"WISDOM IS THE PRINCIPLE THING;
THEREFORE GET WISDOM. AND WITH ALL
THY GETTING, GET UNDERSTANDING"
(PROV. 4:7).

"You can't know everything, so don't even try."

"Believe half of what you see and none of what you hear."

"If you have anything really valuable to contribute to the world, it will come through the expression of your own personality" *(Bruce Barton)*.

"Control what you can control—don't worry about what you can't control."

"You can do bad by yourself; you don't need no help to starve to death."

"If a man dies because of your actions, you can't make it right by him."

"You are opportunity!"

"You are responsible for what you do with your life. No one else" *(Oprah Winfrey)*.

"You don't get a second chance to make a first impression."

"Let the rumors stop with you."

"You should always go to other people's funerals; otherwise, they won't come to yours" *(Yogi Berra, 1925)*.

"Anything that immobilizes me, gets in my way, keeps me from my goals is all mine.

You cannot control what goes on outside, but you can control what goes on inside" *(Wayne Dyer)*.

"If you never change your mind, why have one?" *(Edward D. Bono)*.

"Respect yourself if you would have others respect you."

"Act as if what you do makes a difference. It does" *(William James)*.

"What worries you, masters you" *(John Locke)*.

"You must accept the truth from whatever source that it comes" *(Maimonides, 1135)*.

"Whether you believe you can do a thing or not you are right" *(Horace 65 BC)*.

"The only place where your dreams become impossible is in your own thinking" *(Robert Schuller, 1926)*.

"You can't make yourself happy making other people unhappy."

"When every physical and mental resource is focused, one's power to solve a problem multiplies tremendously" *(Norman Vincente Peale, 1898)*.

"When you are content to be simply yourself and don't compare or compete, everybody will respect you.

"Great things are made up of small deeds" *(Lao Tzu)*.

"You should examine yourself daily. If you find faults, you should correct them. If you find none, you should try even harder" *(Xi Zhi)*.

"Practice yourself in the little thing, and then proceed to the greater" *(Epictelus, 480 BC)*.

"Never take a wife until you have a house to put her in."

"Do not fear mistakes, you will know failure, continue to reach out."

"By failing to prepare, you are preparing to fail."

"He that rises late must trot all day."

"He that speaks much is much mistaken."

"He that would live in peace and ease must not speak all of what he knows or sees" *(Benjamin Franklin, 1706).*

ALPHA OMEGA
"You can make many plans, but the Lord's purpose will prevail" (Prov. 19:21).

"Watch your tongue and keep your mouth shut and you will stay out of trouble" (Prov.21:23).

"If you insult your father or your mother your light will be snuffed out" (Prov. 20:20).

"You can turn a painful situation around through laughter. If you can find humor in anything, even poverty, you can survive it" *(Bill Cosby, 1937).*

"No matter how dressed up you are, the shoes will make or break the outfit."

"You can have anything you want if you give up the belief that you can't have it" *(Robert Anthony)*.

"Hear one side of the story and you will be in the dark, hear both sides and all will be clear."

"Persist and persevere and you will find most things that are unattainable, possible."

"Remember, nothing but strict truth can carry you through the world with your conscience or honor unwounded."

"Whoever is in a hurry shows that the thing that he is about to do is too big for him" *(Lord Chesterfield, 1694)*.

"If you do not conquer self, you will be conquered by self."

"Your big opportunity may be right there where you are."

"He who does not understand your silence probably will not understand your words."

"Know what you want to do, hold the thought firmly, and do everyday what should be done, and every sunset will see you that much closer to you goals."

"The greatest mistake you can make in life is continually fearing that you will make one" *(Elbert Hubbard)*.

"Be careful how you take away hope from another human being."

"Speak clearly if you speak at all; carve every word carefully before you let it fall" *(Oliver Wendell Holmes, 1809)*.

"Be able to confide your inner most secrets to your mother, and your inner most fears to your father."

"Know how your representative stands on major national and state issues."

"When your spelling is perfect, it is invisible. But when it is flawed, it prompts strong negative associations" *(Marilyn vos Savant)*.

"Until you value yourself, you won't value your time. Until you value your time, you won't do anything with it" *(M. Scott Peck)*.

"Pay attention to your body. Don't let it get away from you. It will take you places and do things that you shouldn't. Keep it under subjection."

"Society attacks early when the individual is helpless" *(B.F. Skinner)*.

"Better to remain silent, better not to think, if you are not prepared to act" *(Annie Besant)*.

"The less you open your heart to others the more your heart suffers" *(Deepak Chopra)*.

"If what you have done is unjust, you will not succeed" *(Thomas Carlyle)*.

"A snow goose needs no bath to make itself white. Neither need you do anything but be yourself" *(Laotse)*.

"The more you learn if you learn it properly, the more clear you become, and the more you know" *(Leonard Perkoff, 1909)*.

"If you do not know the law of right conduct, you cannot form good character" *(Swami Sivantanda)*.

"When you give to others, the desires of your enemies against you melt away. Most of your problems are there because you are stingy. *You are not powerless. (Eddie Long)*.

"You have a right to be happy."

"If you serve for the joy of serving, prosperity shall flow to you in unending streams of plenty" *(Charles Fillmore, 1854)*.

"Whoever you are and whatever you are doing, some kind of excellence is within your reach" *(Paula Freire, 1921)*.

"I am the greatest; I said that even before I knew I was"*(Muhammad Ali, 1942)*.

"Focus on the journey not the destination. Joy is found not in finishing, but by doing" *(Greg Anderson, 1964)*.

"Self respect is the fruit of discipline; the sense of dignity grows with the ability to say no to yourself" *(Abraham Joshua Hershel, 1907)*.

"Think for yourself and question authority" *(Timothy Leary, 1920)*.

"Doing nothing for others is the undoing of yourself. Be ashamed to die unless you have won some victory for humanity" *(Horace Mann, 1796)*.

"Character is power."

"Associate yourself with people of quality."

"There are two ways of exerting one's strength; one is pushing down and the other is pulling up" *(Booker T. Washington, 1856)*.

"Every problem has a gift for you in its hand" *(Richard Bach, 1936)*.

"Nothing will work unless you do" *(Maya Angelou)*.

"Your attitude changes your perception about yourself."

"If you are the master be sometimes blind; if you are the servant be sometimes deaf" *(R. Buckminster Fuller, 1895)*.

"Maturity is the ability to reap without apology and not complain when things don't go well."

"Part of your heritage in this society is the opportunity to become financially independent."

"When you know what you want, and want it bad enough, you will find a way to get it."

"You cannot change your destination overnight, but you can change direction overnight."

"Your philosophy will determine whether you will go for the discipline or continue in error" *(Jim Rohn, 1930)*.

"Keeping score of old scars, getting even and one-upping, always makes you less than what you are" *(Malcolm Forbes, 1917)*.

"If you see yourself as prosperous, you will be. If you see yourself as hard up, that's exactly what you will be."

"You have to sow before you can reap; you have to give before you get" *(Robert Collier)*.

"If you can't take it, you won't make it."

"The yoke you wear determines the burden you bear" *(Edwin Louis Cole)*.

"It's not the world that is your oppressor, because what the world does to you, if the world does it to you long enough and effectively enough, you begin to do it to yourself" *(James Baldwin, 1924)*.

"When you can't solve a problem, manage it."

"The truth is, you always know the right thing to do. The hard part is doing it" *(Robert Schuller, 1926)*.

"If you have zest and enthusiasm, you attract zest and enthusiasm."

"You tend to get what you expect" *(Norman Vincente Peale, 1898)*.

"It hurts you when you don't like somebody; it doesn't hurt them."

"Don't worry about the wind; adjust your sail" *(Ted Turner)*.

"Hold yourself responsible to a higher standard than anybody expects of you. Never excuse yourself."

"You are rich or poor according to what you are, not what you have."

"The difference between perseverance and obstinacy is that one comes from a strong will, and the other comes from a strong won't" *(Henry Ward Beecher).*

"If you have an appointment with someone, you owe them punctuality. You have no right to throw away their time like your own" *(Richard Cecil, 1748).*

"Hatred is self-punishment" *(Hosea Ballou, 1771).*

"If your daily life seems poor, do not blame it, blame yourself that you are not poet enough to call forth its riches; for the Creator there is no poverty."

"Perhaps all dragons in our lives are princesses who are only waiting to see us once beautiful and brave" *(Rainer Maria Rilke).*

"If you don't like something change it. If you can't change it, change your attitude" *(Maya Angelou).*

"Youth is a time for getting; middle age is time for improving; and old age a time for spending" *(Anne Bradstreet).*

"Use the talents that you have; for the world would be very silent if no birds sang but the best" *(Henry Van Dyke).*

"We dance and suppose, but the secret sits in the middle and knows" *(Robert Frost).*

"It is better able to retract what you did not say, than what you did" *(Solomon Ion Gabirol, 1021).*

"Tell me and I forget, show me and I remember, involve me and I understand" *(John Gay).*

"Be above it! Make the world serve your purpose, but do not serve its."

"Error is acceptable as long as you are young; but you must not drag it along into old age."

There is nothing more shameful than establishing oneself on lies and fables" *(Johann Wolfgang von Goethe)*.

"He knows not his own strength that has not met adversity" *(Ben Johnson, 1572)*.

"If you don't want to work, you have to work to earn enough money so that you don't have to work" *(Ogden Nash)*.

"Change your opinion, keep your principles; change your leaves, keep intact your roots" *(Victor Hugo)*.

"Better three hours too soon than a minute too late."

"Give every man your ear, but few thy voice" *(William Shakespeare, 1564)*.

"Make yourself necessary to somebody" *(Ralph Waldo Emerson, 1803)*.

"Whoever degrades another degrades you" *(Walt Whitman, 1819)*.

"Do what you can with what you have where you are."

"Nobody cares how much you know until they know how much you care."

"Speak softly and carry a big stick; you will go far" *(Theodore Roosevelt, 1858)*.

"Eating your words won't give you indigestion."

"The farther backwards you look, the farther forward you see" *(Winston Churchill, 1874).*

"The easiest person to deceive is oneself" *(Robert Bulwer Lytton, 1803).*

"You can't know too much, but you can say too much" *(Calvin Coolidge, 1872).*

"Chop your own wood and it will warm you twice" *(Henry Ford, 1863).*

"It doesn't matter who you are, or where you come from, the ability to triumph begins with you. *(Oprah Winfrey).*

"Whatever advice you give, be short" *(Horace, 65 BC).*

"There is no witness so terrible and no accuser so powerful as conscience, which dwells within us" *(Sophocles, 496 BC).*

"The clearer your goals, the greater your faith" *(Pinder, 552 BC).*

"What you can walk away from is mastered, what you can't walk away from has mastered you" *(Pastor Mike Murdock).*

"Reject your sense of injury and the injury itself disappears."

"Waste no time arguing what a good man should be. Be one" *(Plutarch, 46 BC).*

"He who has lost honor can lose nothing more."

"Take care that no man hates you justly" *(Publitius Syrus, 85 BC)*.

"You need to overcome the tug of people against you as you reach for high goals" *(George Patton, 1825)*.

"The best luck of all is the luck you make for yourself" *(Douglas MacArthur, 1880)*.

"Have patience with all things, but first of all with yourself."

"Never undervalue any person. The workman loves not that his work be despised in his presence.

God is everywhere and every man is his work" *(Saint Francis de Sales, 1567)*.

"Deal with the faults of others as gently as with your own" *(Chinese Proverb)*.

"You become responsible for whatever you have tamed."

"To be a man is precisely, to be responsible" *(Antoine de Saint-Exupery, 1900)*.

"No one can disgrace us but ourselves" *(Josh Billing, 1818)*.

"You can't do everything by yourself; don't be afraid to ask for help" *(Winifred Clayton)*.

"Deceive not thy physician, confessor, nor lawyer" *(George Herbert, 1593)*.

"You can never get enough of what you don't need to make you happy" *(Eric Hoffer, 1902)*.

"When you have nothing to say, say nothing" *(Charles Caleb Colton, 1780)*.

"It is not only what we do, but what we do not do for which we are accountable" *(Moliere, 1622)*.

"You should not only use all the brain that you have, but all you can borrow" *(Woodrow Wilson, 1856)*.

"You must have a strong mind ready to accept facts as they are."

"You must pay the price if you wish to secure the blessing" *(Andrew Jackson, 1767)*.

"Don't write so you can be understood; write so you can't be misunderstood" *(William Taft 1857)*.

"Don't wish it was easier, wish you were better."

"Give whatever you are doing and whoever you are with the gift of your attention."

"How long should you try? Until."

"If you are not willing to risk the unusual, you will have to settle for the ordinary."

"If you don't like how things are—change it! You are not a tree" *(Jim Rohn, 1930)*.

"Shouldn't anybody beat you, being confident about you" *(Baron Hopgood)*.

"He is a friend that speaks well of me behind my back."

"Get the facts or they will get you. And when you get them, get them right or they will get you wrong" *(Thomas Fuller, 1608)*.

"If you are not too large for the place you occupy, you are too small for it" *(James Garfield, 1831)*.

"No matter what you do, there will always be someone that is unhappy with you" *(Gary Oliver)*.

"No matter what decision you make good or bad no matter what people say, you only truly have an audience of One.

The very thing that God gave us to hold us together (our skin) is the very thing that divides us (our color)" *(J. C. Watts)*.

"If you are convinced that you are 100% right, be prepared to apologize."

"Allow yourself to see things as they really are. Don't lie to yourself." *(E.A.F.)*.

"When you say, 'if you had not done this, I wouldn't have done that, you have just put yourself in a helpless situation, control yourself."

"When you belong to a minority, you have to be better in order to have the right to be equal" *(Christiane Collage)*.

"You bowed down yesterday, so you will bow down today. You have to come to the point where your integrity is not for sale."

"You should never be intimidated by anything that comes against you" *(Bridget Hilliard)*.

"You have creatorial power within you, you must use it" *(Donnie McClurkin)*.

"Identify yourself with the hopes, dreams, fears, and longings of others, that you may understand them and help them" *(Wilfred Peterson)*.

"In prosperity your friends know you; in adversity you know your friends" *(Steve Harvey)*.

OMEGA

"HONOR YOUR MOTHER AND FATHER THAT YOUR DAYS MAY BE LONG ON THE EARTH" (EXODUS 20:12).

*never ... always ...
sometimes ... don't ...
nothing ...*

ALPHA
"BE QUICK TO HEAR,
SLOW TO SPEAK AND SLOW TO WRATH"
(JAS 1:19).

"Always tell the Lord thank you."

"Never rush into folly just because others people are practicing it" *(Leon Koss, 1939)*.

"Always take care of your babysitter and you won't have a problem with babysitting" *(Dale Mcdade)*.

"Don't go looking for trouble, because you'll find more trouble than you are looking for" *(Michelle Crater, 1962)*.

"Never trust a man that won't look you in the eye."

"Never share your weakness with anybody unless you have already conquered it. Be sure to always give attention where attention is needed." *(E.A.F.)*.

"Sometimes you have to encourage yourself."

"Never be the first to a party or the last to leave."

"Always where quality shoes, your feet will bless you in your latter days."

"Never get mad over another man's money" *(Delois Spencer)*.

"Never loan money that you can't afford to be paid back."

"Always watch the candy man around your children, friend or relative" *(Delois Ford, 1967)*.

"Never leave your kids alone with strangers."

"Never put off till tomorrow what you can do today" *(Thomas Jefferson, 1743)*.

"Always be a father of unconditional love" *(George W. Bush, 1946).*

"Never forget that nearly everything that Hitler did was legal (the law is not always right)" *(Martin Luther King Jr., 1929).*

"Never negotiate out of fear" *(John F. Kennedy, 1917).*

"Never contend with a man that has nothing to lose."

"Never do anything when you are in a temper, for you will do everything wrong" *(Baltasar Gracian, 1601).*

"I never did anything worth doing by accident, nor did any of my inventions come by accident, they came by work" *(Plato, 427 BC).*

"It's important that you complete everything that you start" *(Tyler Perry).*

"Sometimes, and in some situations to do nothing is right, and indeed you will be doing something."

"Never let the facts get in the way of the truth."

"Always respect authority, and you will save yourself a lot of heartache and pain" *(E.A.F.).*

"Martyrs my friend have to choose between being forgotten, mocked, or used. As for being understood—never" *(Albert Camus).*

"Never reach out your hand unless you are willing to extend your arm" *(Pope Paul VI, 1887).*

"Speak the truth to power"

"Never, ever, ever, deny God!"

"Never do anything against conscience even if the state demands it" *(Albert Einstein, 1879)*.

"Don't reject help and conversation, suffering silently is not healthy. Accept support from friends and family."

"Never give an order that cannot be obeyed" *(Douglas McArthur, 1880)*.

"Never confuse motion with action" *(Benjamin Franklin, 1706)*.

"Every closed eye is not sleeping, and every open eye is not seeing" *(Bill Cosby, 1937)*.

"Always be found doing what you're suppose to be doing" *(James Williams)*.

"Always remember that when you love someone that love lasts forever- not part time love" *(Delois Smith Ford)*.

"There is always room at the top" *(Daniel Webster)*.

"Never seek revenge the same way that you were hurt; success is the best revenge" *(Clyde Kennedy)*.

"Don't wait. The time will never be just right."

"The less one has to do, the less time one finds to do it" *(Lord Chesterfield, 1694)*.

"Never put a question mark where God put a period."

"Every calling is great when greatly pursued" *(Oliver Wendell Holmes, 1809)*.

"Sometimes you will do all the right things and still get a bad result."

"Always and never are two words you should remember always never to use" *(Wendell Johnson)*.

"Don't suffer fools gladly."

"A strong mind always has hope, and always has cause to hope" *(Thomas Carlyle)*.

"Don't make a perfect enemy of the good."

"Hope of ill gain is the beginning of loss" *(Democritus, 460 BC)*.

"Don't accept no from someone that doesn't have the power to say yes" *(Otonya Allen)*.

"Words are a potent weapon for all causes good and bad" *(Manly Hall, 1901)*.

"Don't stay in a relationship with anybody that doesn't want to be with you."

"If things go wrong, don't go with them" *(Roger Babson)*.

"I let no man drag me down so low as to make me hate him" *(Booker T. Washington, 1856)*.

"Don't be afraid you'll make a wrong decision, just be ready to deal with the consequences" *(Vickie Westbrook)*.

"Avoid problems and you will never be the one that overcame them."

"Your only obligation in any lifetime is to be true to yourself."

"Get this in your mind early, you never grow up" *(Richard Bach, 1936).*

"Don't have a pity party when you are trying to have a party."

"Anything that you can see you can seize."

"You must never be afraid of a challenge."

"Don't live by superstition" *(Baron Hopgood).*

"Don't stay in bed unless you can make money in bed.
    Nature never breaks her own laws" *(Leonardo da Vinci, 1452).*

"Don't try to take on a new personality, it does not work" *(Richard Nixon, 1913).*

"Never hire a man that knows less than you do about what he is hired to do."

"Never trust a man to control others who cannot control himself."

"Never do a wrong thing to make a friend or keep one" *(Robert E. Lee, 1807).*

"Everything has its wonders, even darkness, and silence. I learn whatever state I may be in therein to be content."

"It is hard to interest those who have everything in those who have nothing."

"Never bend your head. Always hold it high, look the world straight in the eye."

"You're never down, you're either up or getting up" *(John Maxwell)*.

"Optimism is the faith that leads to achievement. Nothing can be done without hope and confidence" *(Helen Keller, 1880)*.

"Truth cannot be defeated."

"When the pressure is on, preferences give way while convictions hold firm" *(Edwin Lewis Cole, 1922)*.

"Hatred which could destroy so much, never failed to destroy the man who hated and this is an immutable law."

"There is never a time in the future in which we will work out salvation. The challenge is in the moment, the time is always now" *(James Baldwin, 1924)*.

"Don't talk people into staying if they want to leave, sometimes there is the gift of good-bye" *(Joel Olsteen)*.

"Do not tell secrets to those whose faith and silence you have not already tested" *(Elizabeth I, 1533)*.

NEVER...ALWAYS...SOMETIMES...DON'T...NOTHING...

ALPHA OMEGA

"DON'T BEFRIEND ANGRY PEOPLE OR
ASSOCIATE WITH HOT-TEMPERED PEOPLE OR
YOU WILL LEARN TO BE LIKE THEM"
(PROV. 22:24–25).

"SO IT IS WITH THE MAN WHO SLEEPS
WITH ANOTHER MAN'S WIFE, HE THAT
EMBRACES HER WILL NOT GO UNPUNISHED"
(PROV. 6:29).

"Heaven never helps the men who will not act" *(Sydney Smith)*.

"Always look at what you have left. Never look at what you have lost."

"Never underestimate your problem or your ability to deal with it."

"It is better to do something imperfectly than to do nothing flawlessly."

"Tough times never last, tough people do."

"You never suffer a money problem; you suffer from a idea problem" *(Robert Schuller, 1926)*.

"Sometimes you'll want something bad enough to realize that you don't need it."

"Don't take tomorrow to bed with you."

"Empty pockets never held anyone back. Only empty heads and empty hearts can do that."

"Never say anything to hurt anyone. You are to refrain from double talk. You are to turn your back on evil, and in every way possible do good, help people and bring blessings into their lives" *(Norman Vincent Peale, 1898)*.

"Never forget what a man says to you when he is angry."

"You never know the love of a parent until you become a parent yourself."

"We should never judge a man by their peak of excellence; but by the distance they traveled from the point where they started" *(Henry Ward Breecher)*.

"Never chase a lie. Let it alone and it will run itself to death" *(Lyman Beecher, 1775)*.

"You'll never get a perfect job out of an imperfect man" *(E.A.F.)*.

"Don't simply retire from something, have something to retire to" *(Henry Emerson Fosdick, 1869)*.

"Never believe anything bad about anybody unless you positively know it to be true; never to tell even that unless you feel it is absolutely necessary, and remember that God is listening" *(Henry Van Dyke)*.

"Death never takes the wise man by surprise; he is always ready to go" *(Jean de la Fontaine, 1621)*.

"Whoever wishes to keep a secret must hide the fact that he has one" *(Johann Wolfgang Von Goethe, 1749)*.

"In a full heart there is room for everything; in a empty heart there is room for nothing" *(Antonio Purchia, 1885)*.

"Never ignore a gut feeling, but never believe that it is enough" *(Robert Heller, 1826)*.

"Good enough never is" *(Debbie Fields, 1956)*.

"We may encounter many defeats, but we must not be defeated" *(Maya Angelou)*.

"Don't ever take a fence down, until you know why it was put up" *(Robert Frost, 1963)*.

"Never hold a discussion with the monkey when the organ grinder is in the room" *(Winston Churchill, 1874)*.

"Don't expect to build up the weak by pulling down the strong" *(Calvin Coolidge, 1872)*.

"It is always better to have no ideas than false ones; believe nothing, than to believe what is wrong" *(Thomas Jefferson, 1743)*.

"Victory has a thousand fathers, defeat is an orphan" *(John F. Kennedy, 1917)*.

"A man that authority is recent is always stern."

"Time as he grows teaches all things" *(Aeschylus, 525 BC)*.

"Never interrupt your enemy when he is making a mistake" *(Napoleon Bonaparte, 1769)*.

"Never permit ourselves to do anything that we are not willing to see our children do" *(Brigham Young, 1801)*.

"Never let your sight limit your vision" *(Maya Angelou)*.

"Authority is never without hate."

"Cleverness is not wisdom."

"Don't consider painful what is good for you."

"No one who lives in error is free" *(Euripides, 480 BC)*.

"A lie never lives to be old" *(Sophocles, 496 BC)*.

"The best healer is good cheer" *(Pinder, 552 BC)*.

"It is better to learn late than never."

"Never promise more than you can perform" *(Publilius Syrus, 85 BC)*.

"Everything comes to him who hustles while he waits" *(Thomas Edison, 1847)*.

"If you leave your drink unattended don't drink it when you return" *(Rosie Ford)*.

"This is the first fault of wine, it first trips up the feet; it is a cunning wrestler."

"A mouse never entrusts his life to one hole."

"Things are not always what they seem; the first appearance deceives many" *(Titus Maccius Plautus, 254 BC)*.

"Never help a child with a task at which he feels he can succeed" *(Maria Montessori, 1870)*.

"He who stops being better, stops being good" *(Oliver Cromwell, 1599)*.

"Never stand begging for what you have the power to earn" *(Miguel de Cervantes, 1547)*.

"Don't take the wrong side of an argument just because your opponent took the right side."

"Never open the door to a lesser evil, for other greater ones invariably slink in after it" *(Baltasar Gracian, 1601)*.

"Nothing is so strong as gentleness, nothing so gentle as real strength" *(Saint Francis de Sales, 1567)*.

"A friendship that can cease, has never been real" *(St. Jerome, 340)*.

"Don't set your wits against a child" *(Jonathan Swift, 1667)*.

"Never find fault with the absent" *(Alexander Pope, 1688)*.

"Never be bullied into silence. Never allow yourself to be made a victim. Accept no one's definition of your life, define yourself" *(Harvey Fierstein, 1954)*.

"Remember the poor; it costs you nothing" *(Josh Billing, 1818)*.

"Don't drink the third glass, which thou canst tame, when once it is within thee" *(George Herbert, 1593)*.

"Don't make the mistake of thinking that you have to agree with people, and their beliefs to defend them from injustice" *(Bryant H. Hill)*.

"Drink because you are happy, not because you are miserable" *(Gilbert K. Chisterson)*.

"Be a one-woman man" *(W.C. Davis, 1928)*.

"Always be sincere even if you don't mean it" *(Harry Truman, 1884)*.

"Don't just read the easy stuff, you may be entertained by it, but you will never grow from it.

Don't wish it were easier, wish you were better" *(Jim Rohn, 1930)*.

"A word once uttered can never be recalled" *(Horace, 65 BC)*.

"Chance is always powerful; let your hook always be cast in the pool where you least expect there will be fish" *(Ovid, 43 BC)*.

"Nothing comes to a sleeper but a dream" *(Sherman Sprinkle)*.

"Never let all your assumptions be negative."

"Don't run after the arsonist, put out the fire first. Take control of yourself first."

"Don't be bitter; be better."

"Your faith will never rise above the level of your confession."

"Faith cometh by hearing, even if the Word comes out of your own mouth" *(Fredrick K.C. Price)*.

"A closed mouth will never be fed."

"Never force folks to stay on a train who are not going to your destination" *(Freddie Haynes)*.

"Never peer through windows on matters that don't concern you."

"Always be alert to all that goes on around you: that you may build an ever increasing knowledge of the universe."

"Enlarge the scope of your life through the expansion of your personality."

"We always believe others to be happier than they really are."

OMEGA
"NEVER ABANDON A FRIEND,
EITHER YOURS OR YOUR FATHER'S"
(PROV. 27:10).

people ...friends ...
foes ...family ...

ALPHA

THE GLORY OF THE FATHER IS HIS WIFE;
THE GLORY OF THE WIFE IS HER HAIR;
THE GLORY OF THE CHILD IS THE FATHER
(1 COR. 11:7, 11:15; PROV. 17:6).

"Know your opponent."

"Bad little boys grow up to be bad men if left unchecked."

"Scratch a lie, find a thief."

"Life is a battle a wills, one trying to dominate the other"
(E.A.F.).

"A child spells love t.i.m.e."

"The best place to hide information from some people
is to put it in a book."

"Now that you have two meats on your table, don't forget where you came from.
    Nobody appreciates being forgotten for the deeds
that they have done" *(Anthony Wilcox).*

"People are lonely because they build walls instead of
bridges."

"Remember, your enemy has to bring some, to get some"
(Battle).

"The most you can do for a friend is simply be a friend"
(Henry David Thoreau).

"Forgive your enemies, but never for get their names"
(John F. Kennedy, 1917).

ALPHA OMEGA

"Do not plot harm against thy neighbor
for those who live near by trust you"
(Prov. 3:29).

"A lazy person is as bad as
someone that destroys things"
(Prov. 18:9).

"A wise child brings joy to a father, a
foolish child brings grief to a mother"
(Prov. 15:20).

"People with integrity walk safely,
but those who follow crooked paths
will slip and fall"
(Prov. 10:20).

"A gossip goes around telling secrets,
but those who are trustworthy
can keep a confidence"
(Prov. 11:13).

"The rich pay a ransom for their lives,
but the poor won't even be threatened"
(Prov. 13:8).

"PEOPLE WITH UNDERSTANDING
CONTROL THEIR ANGER, A HOT TEMPER
SHOWS GREAT FOOLISHNESS"
(PROV. 14:28).

"A FRIEND IS ALWAYS LOYAL AND A BROTHER
IS BORN TO HELP IN A TIME OF NEED"
(PROV. 17:17).

"Many have had their greatness made for them by their enemies" *(Baltasar Gracian, 1601)*.

"A friend to all is a friend to none" *(Aristotle, 384 BC)*.

"A person attempting to travel two roads at once will get nowhere" *(Xi Zhi)*.

"There are two things a person should not be angry at, what they can help and what they cannot" *(Plato, 427 BC)*.

"Don't walk behind me, I may not lead, don't walk in front of me, I may not follow, just walk beside me and be my friend."

"Man is the only creature that refuses to be what he is" *(Albert Camus)*.

"A friend is one who comes in when the whole world has gone out."

"Great leaders always offer solutions that everyone can understand" *(Colin Powell)*.

"Remember, whenever you get around family, you can find love."

"If a man does not keep pace with his companions, perhaps it is because he hears a different drummer" *(Henry David Thoreau, 1817)*.

"Give people a reputation to uphold" *(John Maxwell)*.

"Be there for the child regardless of the differences that you have with the parent."

"A drowning person will fight you because you are a sign of life. Don't give up on people.

"Even all cleaned up people can still see your dirt" *(Ricky Rush)*.

"Invest in building relationships, start building up others" *(Fredrick Bennett)*.

"A person that never made a mistake, never tried anything."

"Everyone should be respected as an individual, but no one should be idolized" *(Albert Einstein, 1879)*.

"No palace is safe when the cottage is not happy."

"Be slow in choosing a friend and even slower in changing" *(Benjamin Franklin, 1706)*.

"Some people will only listen to you, so push them in the right direction" *(JoAnn Hardnett)*.

"Sometimes all you need to do is talk over a problem with a friend to help put it in perspective."

"An injury is much sooner forgotten than an insult" *(Daniel Webster)*.

"With friends new is good, old is best."

"A bullet doesn't have people names on it when fired."

"Men as well as women are much often led by their hearts, than by their understanding."

"You must look into people as well as at them" *(Lord Chesterfield, 1694)*.

"Effort only fully releases its reward after a person refuses to quit."

"Man alone has the power to transform his thoughts into physical reality, and make his dreams come true."

"More gold has been mined from the thoughts of men than has been taken from the earth."

"The world has a way of making room for the person whose actions shows they know where they are going" *(Napoleon Hill)*.

"There are plenty of roses, stars, sunsets, rainbows, brothers and sisters, aunts and uncles, but only one mother in the whole world" *(Kate Douglas)*.

"A man is not paid for having a head and a hand but for using them."

"Men are only as great as they are kind."

"Reversing the treatment of a man you have wronged is better than asking for forgiveness."

"A friend is someone who knows all about you and still loves you" *(Elbert Hubbard)*.

"The young man knows the rules, but the old man knows the exception" *(Oliver Wendell Holmes)*.

"He who is reluctant to recognize me opposes me" *(Frantz Fanon)*.

"Women wish to be loved without a why or a wherefore; but because they are themselves" *(Henry Frederic Amiel)*.

"People put a pretty face on things so that they don't have to deal with what it really is" *(Chasety Bennett)*.

"Of all the acts of man, repentance is the most divine" *(Thomas Carlyle)*.

"Stay," is a charming word in a friend's vocabulary."

"The less a man thinks the more they talk" *(Charles de Montesquieu)*.

"Relationships: You cannot go back and have a new start, but you can start now and have a new ending" *(Sheryl Modester, 1968)*.

"Never are so empty as those who are full of themselves" *(Benjamin Whichcote, 1683)*.

"Many people lose their tempers merely from seeing you keep yours" *(Frank Moore Colby, 1865)*.

"The efficient is a man that thinks for himself" *(Charles Eliot, 1834)*.

"We increase whatever we praise. The whole creation responds to praise and is glad" *(Charles Fillmore, 1854)*.

"If you have some respect for people as they are, you can be more effective in helping them become better than they are."

"One of the reasons people stop learning is that they become less and less willing to risk failure" *(John W. Gardner, 1912)*.

"Dignity is not negotiable. Dignity is honor of the family" *(Vartan Gregorian, 1934)*.

"I know I got it made while the mass of black people are catching hell, but as long as they ain't free, I ain't free" *(Muhammad Ali, 1942)*.

"Racism is man's gravest threat to man—the maximum of hatred for the minimum of reasons."

"The test of the people or person is how it behaves toward the old. It is easy to love children."

"Man is a messenger who forgot the message" *(Abraham Joshua Herschel, 1907)*.

"Leaders establish the vision for the future and set the strategy for getting there" *(John Kotter, 1920)*.

"Many people die at twenty-five and aren't buried until seventy-five" *(Robert M. Hutchins, 1899).*

"Boldness be my friend."

"'Tis best to weigh the enemy more mightily than he seems" *(William Shakespeare, 1564).*

"Face it! Some people simply do not pack fair" *(Michael L. Gee).*

"A man should keep his friendships in constant repair."

"It matters not how a man dies but how he lives" *(Samuel Johnson, 1709).*

"It is the first duty of man not to be poor" *(George Bernard Shaw).*

"In war you can only be killed once, but in politics many times."

"You have enemies? Good. That means you've stood up for something, sometime in your life" *(Winston Churchill, 1874).*

"Every man that observes vigilantly and resolves steadfastly grows unconsciously into genius."

"When a man is down in the world, an ounce of help is better than a pound of preaching."

"Whatever the number of a man's friends, there will be times when he has one too few" *(Robert Bulwer-Lytton, 1803).*

"Only a stomach that rarely feels hunger scorns common things."

"Avoid inquisitive persons, for they are sure for gossip. They will not keep what is entrusted to them" *(Horace, 65 BC).*

"There is no man living that cannot do more than he thinks he can" *(Henry Ford, 1863).*

"Every man is surrounded by a neighborhood of volunteer spies" *(Jane Austen).*

"Forgive son, men are men they need must err."

"Friends show their love in times of trouble."

"One loyal friend is worth ten thousand relatives."

"To a father growing old there is nothing dearer than a daughter."

"When a man's stomach is full it makes no difference if he is rich or poor" *(Euripides, 480 BC).*

"When a man has lost all happiness, he is not alive—call him a corpse" *(Sophocles, 496 BC).*

"The more one judges, the less one loves" *(Honore de Balzac).*

"Admonish your friends privately, but praise them openly."

"From the errors of others a wise man corrects his own."

"The person who receives the most favors is the one who knows how to return them" *(Publilius, 85 BC).*

"You can take a chance on a man that pays his bills on time" *(Terrence, 170 BC).*

"Everyone is bound to bear, patiently the results of his own example" *(Phaedrus, 15 BC).*

"You cannot teach a man anything; you can only help him discover it within himself" *(Galileo Galilei, 1564).*

"If a man does his best, what else is there?" *(George Patton, 1885).*

"True friendship should never conceal what it thinks."

"The scars of others teach you caution" *(St Jerome, 420).*

"People seldom improve when they have no other model but themselves to copy after" *(Oliver Goldsmith, 1730).*

"Fools rush in where angels fear to tread" *(Alexander Pope, 1688).*

"The best way to convince a fool that he is wrong is to let him have his own way."

"There are some people so addicted to exaggeration that they can't tell the truth without lying" *(Josh Billing, 1818).*

"Every man's work, whether it be literature, or music, or pictures, or architecture, or anything else is always a portrait of himself" *(Samuel Butler).*

"Power always thinks it has a great soul and a vast view beyond the comprehension of the weak" *(John Adams, 1735).*

"Anyone that can walk to the welfare office can walk to work" *(Al Capp)*.

"Don't allow people to polarize you and shrink you (that may be their strategy to defeat you)" *(Newt Gingrich)*.

"The few who do are the envy of the many who only watch" *(Jim Rohn, 1930)*.

"People blame their environment. There is only one person to blame and only one—themselves" *(Robert Collier)*.

"Many people know so little about what is beyond their short range of experience. They look within themselves and find nothing. Therefore, they conclude that there is nothing outside themselves either.

People don't like to think, if one thinks, one must reach conclusions. Conclusions are not always pleasant" *(Helen Keller, 1880)*.

"Don't embarrass the family name" *(Kimberly Waller)*.

"Being faithful in that which belongs to another man, qualifies us to receive our own."

"Good is the enemy of best."

"Inconsistencies of men are generally testimony to their immaturity."

"You can tell the nature of a man by the words he chooses."

"Your best friend and worst enemy are both in this room

right now. It's not your neighbor, God, or the devil. It's you" *(Edwin Louis Cole, 1922).*

"Children have not been very good at listening to their elders, but they have never failed to imitate them."

"People can cry much easier than they can change."

"Anyone who has ever struggled with poverty knows how expensive it is to be poor" *(James Baldwin, 1924).*

ALPHA OMEGA
"PEOPLE RUIN THEIR OWN LIVES BY THEIR OWN FOOLISHNESS AND THEN ARE ANGRY AT THE LORD" (PROV. 19:3).

"CHILDREN BORN TO A YOUNG MAN ARE LIKE ARROWS IN A WARRIOR'S HAND. HOW JOYFUL IS THE MAN WHOSE QUIVER IS FULL OF THEM!" (PS. 127:4,5).

"A man is not good or bad for one action."

"Compliments cost nothing yet many pay dearly for them" *(Thomas Fuller, 1608).*

"The problem with most of us is that we would rather be ruined by praise than saved by criticism. A man that does not know how to be angry, does not know how to be good" *(Norman Vincente Peale, 1898).*

"A real man always find excuses for others, but never for himself" *(Henry Ward Beecher)*.

"No man can harm a man who does himself no wrong" *(Chrysostom)*.

"Know that you are your greatest enemy, but also your greatest friend."

"Secrecy is the chastity of friendship" *(Jeremy Taylor, 1613)*.

"If people can see that you love them, you can say anything to them" *(Robin Baxter, 1615)*.

"People buy into the leader before they buy into the vision" *(John Maxwell, 1947)*.

"A man is not complete until he has seen the baby he has made" *(Sammy Davis Jr., 1925)*.

"Men of their senses learn from their enemies. It is from their foes not their friends that cities learn the lesson of building high walls and ships of war" *(Aristophanes, 448)*.

"Hungry men reach for the book, not the weapon" *(Bertolt Brecht)*.

"Fate chooses our relatives, we choose our friends" *(Jacque Delille, 1738)*.

"Let's tell the young people the best books are yet to be written; the best paintings, the best government; the best of everything is to be done by them" *(John Erskine, 1879)*.

"People who make no noise are dangerous" *(Jean de la Fontaine, 1621)*.

"The world is full of willing people; some willing to work, the rest willing to let them" *(Robert Frost, 1874)*.

"Whoever controls the media, the images, controls the culture" *(Allen Ginsberg, 1926)*.

"Men have first class loyalty to second class causes and these causes betray them" *(Lynch Harold Hough)*.

"Sometimes, only one person is missing, and the whole world seems depopulated" *(Alphonse de Lamastine, 1790)*.

"Children are a gift from God; we can learn valuable lessons from their inquisitive minds and trusting hearts. They are not to be treated as a distraction, nuisance or an inconvenience, when God values them so highly."

"A person hears only what they understand."

"Dream no small dreams, for they have no power to move the hearts of men."

"For a man to achieve all that is demanded of him, he must regard himself greater than he is."

"A coward only threatens when he is safe."

"He is happiest, be him king or peasant, who finds peace in his home."

"Ignorant men ask questions that the wise men answered a thousand years ago."

"Self-knowledge comes from knowing other people."

"The little man is still a man" *(Johann Wolfgang von Goethe, 1749)*.

"A good man is better than a bad man. Be him a peasant or a king."

"People hang out with people who support their bad decision-making."

"It's the haters that get you in trouble with the king. The king is too busy. Watch the haters" *(Sherman C. G. Allen)*.

"Family fight for one another; not one another" *(Julius Bradley)*.

"Women minimize and men delete; women have better ability to recall and men have a harder time remembering."

"A great many people think they are thinking, when they are merely rearranging their prejudices" *(William James)*.

"Children are the anchors that holds a mother to life" *(Sophocles, 496 BC)*.

"A child that does not make the mother sleep at night shall not sleep either" *(African Proverb)*.

OMEGA

"AN OFFENDED FRIEND IS AS HARD TO WIN BACK AS A FORTIFIED CITY" (PROV. 18:19).

business ... ideas ...
living ... working ...

ALPHA

"THERE IS DANGER IN PUTTING UP SECURITY
FOR A STRANGER'S DEBT, ITS SAFER NOT
TO GUARANTEE ANOTHER PERSON'S DEBT"
(PROV. 11:15).

"When making your choices in life, do not neglect to live" *(Samuel Johnson, 1709)*.

"When you play, play hard; when you work, don't play at all" *(Theodore Roosevelt, 1859)*.

"Money doesn't talk, it screams" *(Clara Luper)*.

"However beautiful the strategy, you should occasionally look at the results."

"There is no such thing as public opinion. There is only published opinion" *(Winston Churchill, 1874)*.

"Those who trust to chance must abide by the results of chance" *(Calvin Coolidge, 1933)*.

"A man should never neglect his family for business" *(Walt Disney, 1901)*.

"Nothing is particularly hard if you divide it into small jobs."

"Failure is simply an opportunity to begin again; this time more intelligently" *(Henry Ford, 1863)*.

"It is a profitable thing if one is wise to seem foolish" *(Aeschylus, 525 BC)*.

"Labor diligently to increase your property."

"Make good use of the present."

"Money is a handmaiden if thou knowest how to use it; a mistress, if thou knowest not" *(Horace, 65 BC)*.

"If you add a little to a little, and do it often, soon the little will be great."

"When you deal with your brother be pleasant, but get a witness" *(Hesiod, 800 BC).*

"Don't plan for ventures before finishing what's at hand" *(Euripides, 480 BC).*

"If you want to borrow something and not give it back, borrow faith, hope, and love, borrow courage, humility, and integrity, and borrow confidence and strength. Nobody minds; keep them." *(E.A.F)*

"If you take expectation out of your giving, you strip God of your seed."

"Honor is the seed of longevity, in anything" *(Mike Murdock).*

"Poverty is the mother of crime" *(Marcus Aurelius, 121).*

"It is a fraud to borrow what we are unable to pay."

"Practice is the best of all instructors" *(Publilius Syrus, 85 BC).*

"Good merchandise even hidden soon finds buyers" *(Titus Maccius Plautus 254 BC).*

"Take calculated risks; that is far better than being rash" *(George Patton, 1895).*

"A pile of rocks ceases to be rocks when somebody contemplates it with the idea of a cathedral in mind" *(W. H. Auden, 1907).*

"Finances, like time, devours its own children" *(Horace de Balzac, 1799).*

"Sometimes you will have problems that were your own idea" *(Sherman C. G. Allen).*

"A lean compromise is better than a fat lawsuit."

"He that has lost his credit is dead to the world" *(George Herbert, 1593).*

"When a man says 'It ain't about the money but the principle of the thing,' it's the money" *(Kin Hubbard, 1868).*

"Quality is not an accident. It is always the result of intelligent effort" *(John Ruskin, 1819).*

"Time is the scarcest of resources and unless it is managed nothing else can be" *(Peter Drucker, 1909).*

"Don't be afraid to give up the good to go for the great.
    The most important thing for a young person is to establish credit…reputation, character" *(John D. Rockefeller 1838).*

"Labor gives way to ideas" *(Jim Rohn, 1930).*

"If you find something that you love to do, you will never have to go to work."

"There is no substitute for hard work."

"A man that won't work will steal."

"Money doesn't make you; you make money."

"Pay your debts; you did use the money" *(Marjorie Lewis)*.

"Men who accomplish great things in the industrial world are those who have faith in the money producing power of ideas" *(Charles Fillmore, 1854)*.

"Never expect a loan to a friend to be paid back, if you want to keep a friend."

"Take without forgetting and give without remembering" *(Bryant H. Mchill, 1969)*.

"When you get paid, pay yourself—you earned it."

"A man's mind once stretched by an idea never returns to its' former shape"*(Oliver Wendell Holmes,1809)*

"To earn more you must learn more."

"Don't pay for effort, pay for results."

"It's okay sometimes to push back no matter who it is" *(E.A.F, 1964)*.

"All work and no play makes Jack a dull boy; but all play and no work makes him something even worse."

"Learn about the rule of 72."

"He who opens a school door closes a prison."

"It is easy to make a buck. It's a lot harder to make a difference."

"The superior man understands what is right; the inferior man understands what will sell" *(Confucius)*.

"Profit in business comes from repeat customers, customers that boast about your project or service, and bring friends" *(W. Edwards Demming)*.

"Documentation beats conversation" *(Danny Bradley, 1963)*.

"The hardest thing to learn in the world is the income tax" *(Albert Einstein, 1880)*.

"If you don't drive your business, you'll be driven out of business" *(B.C. Forbes)*.

"All lasting business is built on friendship."

"Don't let your ego get to close to your position, so that if your position gets shot down your ego doesn't go with it."

"Your most unhappy customers are your greatest source of learning" *(Bill Gates)*.

"No man can work a man no harder than he wants to be worked."

"Never spend your money before your have earned it" *(Thomas Jefferson, 1743)*.

ALPHA OMEGA
"A LITTLE MORE SLEEP;
A LITTLE EXTRA SLUMBER, THEN POVERTY
WILL POUNCE ON YOU LIKE A BANDIT"
(PROV. 6:11).

"Work expands so as to fill the time available for completion" *(Northcote Parkinson)*.

"Life has to be lived" *(Sydney Portier)*.

"It's never crowded along the extra mile" *(Wayne Dryer)*.

"Opportunity ideas do not lie around waiting to be discovered. Such ideas need to be produced"

"If you wait for opportunity to occur you will be one of the crowd"*(Edward D. Bono)*.

"The only fence against the world is a thorough knowledge of it" *(John Locke, 1632)*.

"Nothing takes the place of persistence."

"Wealth is well known to be a great comforter" *(Plato, 427 BC)*.

"Don't wait for the last judgment; it happens everyday" *(Albert Camus)*.

"You should never feel secure under another man's security. Create your own security.

An idea is more powerful than an army" *(Myles Munroe)*.

"Remember that credit is money."

"Well done is better than well said."

"Who is rich? He that rejoices in his portion."

"Energy and persistence conquers all things."

"A man empties his purse into his head, no one can take it from him."

"If you know how to spend less than you get, you have the philosopher's stone" *(Benjamin Franklin, 1706)*.

"Take care of the minutes and the hours will take care of themselves."

"Knowledge gives weight but accomplishment gives luster, and many more people see than weigh."

"Wear your learning like your watch, in a private pocket. Do not pull it out and strike it merely to show you have one" *(Lord Chesterfield, 1964)*.

"Don't wait for opportunity, make it."

"Do your work with your whole heart, and you will succeed—there is so little competition" *(Elbert Hubbard)*.

"Ideas are the beginning points of all fortunes."

"You gotta make calls to get results" *(Saundra Ford)*.

"Often we can help most by leaving each other alone; at other times we need a grasp hand and a word of cheer."

"The best preparation to do good work tomorrow is to do good work today."

"We work to become not to acquire."

"Death tugs at your ear and says: 'live, I am coming.'"

"Many ideas grow better when planted into another

mind than the one where they sprung up" *(Oliver Wendell Holmes, 1809).*

"If you don't express your original ideas, if you do not listen to your own being, you have betrayed yourself" *(Rollo May).*

"Those who give hoping to be rewarded with honors are not giving; they are bargaining" *(Philo, 20 BC).*

"The only sure weapon against a bad idea is a better idea" *(Alfred Whitney Griswold, 1906).*

"Rich is better than poor."

"If there is a book that you really want to read, but it hasn't been written yet, then you must write it" *(Toni Morrison, 1903).*

"You have to believe in your product."

"If you have to shine shoes, you should look like a million dollars doing it."

"If there is no risk taking in your life, you are not a true entrepreneur."

"Go out and maximize your potential—now is the time, now is the season."

"To maximize your vision do not allow your handicap to cripple you."

"All forces in the world are not so powerful as an idea whose time has come" *(Victor Hugo, 1802).*

"Money is attracted, not pursued."

"Problem solving = what could I do, what could I read? Who could I ask?"

"Work harder on yourself than you do on your job" *(Jim Rohn, 1930).*

"If there is a part of your job that you hate doing, and it has to be done, and it's not going anywhere, make friends with it and get it done" *(James French).*

"Pay your people the least possible and you'll get from them the same" *(Malcolm Forbes, 1917).*

"All riches have their origin in the mind. Wealth is in ideas—not money."

"Make every thought, every fact that comes into your mind pay you a profit. Make it work and produce for you. Think not as they are but as they might be, don't merely dream-but create.

Visualize this thing that you want, see it, feel it, and believe it. Make your mental blueprint, and begin to build" *(Robert Collier).*

"There is a high cost to living low" *(Edwin Louis Cole).*

"Our great lack is not money for any undertaking, but rather ideas. If the ideas are good, cash will somehow flow to where it is needed" *(Saint Francis de Sales, 1567).*

"Do the hard things when times are good. Don't wait for hard times to start a business" *(Michael Baisden)*

"The more you lose yourself in something bigger than yourself, the more energy you will have" *(Norman Vincente Peale, 1898).*

"The ability to convert ideas to things is the secret of the word success" *(Henry Ward Breecher, 1813).*

"One of the secrets to getting things done is a to do list, everyday keep it, keep it visible and use it as a guide to action as you go through your day" *(Jean de la Fontaine, 1621).*

"For just when ideas fail, a word comes in to save the situation."

"In the realm of ideas everything depends on enthusiasm … in the real world all rest on perseverance" *(Johann Wolfgang von Goethe).*

"Where two take counsel there is not lack of plans" *(Silius Halicus, 25 BC).*

"Advertising says to people, 'Here's what we've got. Here's what it will do. Here's how you can get it.'"

"Advertising: Make it simple, make it memorable. Make it inviting to look at. Make it fun to read."

"What helps people helps business" *(Leo Burnett, 1891).*

"He that sells what isn't his must buy it back or go to prison" *(Daniel Drew, 1797).*

"If it is hard then do it hard."

"Buy when others are selling" *(J. Paul Getty, 1892).*

"A verbal contract isn't worth the paper it's printed on" *(Sam Goldwyn, 1879).*

"Every man should make up in his mind that if he expects to succeed, he must give an honest return for the other man's dollar" *(Edward Harriman, 1848).*

"When your work speaks for itself, don't interrupt" *(Henry J. Kaiser, 1882).*

"One of the greatest pains to human nature is the pain of a new idea" *(Walter Bagehot, 1877).*

"You only need one good idea to live like a king the rest of your life" *(Ross Perot).*

"Build a better mousetrap and the world will beat a path to your door" *(Ralph Waldo Emerson, 1803).*

"In order for you to live by your convictions, you must first have some convictions."

"Don't feed other people monkeys—make them do their job instead of you doing some or part for them" *(Michael Holder).*

"The cold war was ended by ideas" *(Ben Wattenberg).*

"Everyone ends up somewhere in life, but very few end up somewhere on purpose" *(Gary Oliver).*

"Those who work the hardest make the most."

"Everyone wants to start out at the top. The only people that start out at the top are the ones that dig holes" *(Cre-flo Dollar).*

"Keep living if you make it through Winter, Spring is coming."

"If you need money, go to work" *(Michael Matthews)*.

"Trust but verify" *(Ronald Reagan, 1911)*.

OMEGA
"WORK BRINGS FORTH PROFIT,
MERE TALK LEADS TO POVERTY"
(PROV. 14:23).

courage ... fear ...
strength ... weakness ...

ALPHA

"FEAR OF THE LORD LENGTHENS
ONE'S LIFE, BUT THE YEARS
OF THE WICKED ARE CUT SHORT"
(PROV. 10:27).

"Cowards die many times before their death; the valiant taste death but once."

"A good head and a good heart are always a formidable combination" *(William Shakespeare, 1564)*.

"Solitary trees, if they grow at all, grow strong."

"Sure I am of this, you have only to endure to conquer."

"We shall draw from the heart of suffering itself the means of inspiration and survival" *(Winston Churchill, 1874)*.

"There is no meeting of the minds, no point of understanding with such terror. Just a choice. Defeat it, or be defeated by it. And defeat it we must" *(Tony Blair)*.

"One man with courage is a majority" *(Thomas Jefferson, 1743)*.

"I'd rather give my life than be afraid to give it" *(Lyndon B. Johnson, 1908)*.

"In a just cause the weak will beat the strong" *(Sophocles, 496 BC)*.

"He that will be angry for anything, will be angry for nothing" *(Sallust, 86 BC)*.

"Evil is always possible, goodness is a difficulty" *(Anne Rice)*.

"If you want to make enemies try to change something." *(Woodrow Wilson, 1856)*

"Rudeness is a weak imitation of strength" *(Eric Hoffer, 1902)*.

"Right reason is stronger than force" *(James Garfield, 1831)*.

"God grant you the strength to fight off the temptation of surrender" *(Walter Annenberg, 1908)*.

"It's not the size of the dog in the fight, but the size of the fight in the dog."

"If a man hasn't found something that he is willing to die for, he is not fit to live" *(Martin Luther King Jr., 1929)*.

"No one can make you feel inferior without your own consent" *(Eleanor Roosevelt)*.

"Don't be afraid to stand alone, be independent."

"Every dragon has a weak spot."

"I can accept failure, but I can't accept not trying" *(Michael Jordan)*.

"Power corrupts, but absolute power corrupts absolutely" *(Lord Acton, 1834)*.

"Get mad then get over it" *(Colin Powell)*.

"Courage is knowing what not to fear" *(Plato, 428)*.

"Have no fear in moving into the unknown" *(Pope John Paul II)*.

"If our women are willing to die with us, who is there to say no?"

"As we must account for every idle word, so must we account for every idle silence" *(Benjamin Franklin, 1706)*.

"Fear is nothing more than a state of mind" *(Napoleon Hill)*.

"No man is ever whipped until he quits in his own mind"

"Have the courage to get instead of react" *(Oliver Wendell Holmes, 1809)*.

"Endurance is patience concentrated" *(Thomas Carlyle)*.

"Mankind fears an evil man, but heaven does not" *(Mencius, 371 BC)*.

"Look at misfortune the same way as success—don't panic!"

"Do your best and forget the consequences" *(Walt Alston, 1911)*.

"It is fatal to enter any war without the will to win it.
    Only those who are fit to live are not afraid to die" *(Douglas McArthur, 1880)*.

"You can measure a man's greatness by how much it takes to discourage him" *(Jim Matnay)*.

"Better to fight for something than live for nothing" *(George Patton, 1885)*.

"Fear attracts attack."

"Prayer in private results in boldness in public" *(Edwin Louis Cole, 1922).*

"Whatever needs to be maintained through force is doomed" *(Henry Miller).*

"A clear and innocent conscience fears nothing" *(Elizabeth I, 1533).*

"He does not believe who does not live according to his belief" *(Thomas Fuller, 1608).*

"Don't lose courage in considering your own imperfections" *(Saint Francis de Sale, 1567).*

"Press on, the problems are seldom the same size tomorrow as they are today" *(Robert Schuller, 1926).*

"Stand up to your own obstacles and do something about them. You will find that they haven't half the strength you think they have."

"You will break the bow if you keep it always stretched" *(Norman Vincente Peale, 1898).*

"We must constantly build the dykes of courage to hold back the flood of fear" *(Martin Luther King Jr.).*

"Hunger knows no friend but its feeder" *(Aristophanes, 448).*

"Strength is a matter of a made up mind" *(John Beecher, 1901).*

"The first virtue of a soldier is to endure fatigue; courage is only the second virtue" *(Napoleon Bonaparte, 1769).*

"The world has no room for cowards; we must all be ready to suffer, to toil, to die" *(Robert Louis Stevenson)*.

"When strong be merciful if you would have respect, not the fear, of your neighbors" *(Chilon)*.

"Our own heart, not another man's opinion, forms our true honor" *(Samuel Taylor Coleridge, 1772)*.

"Knowing is not enough; we must apply. Willing is not enough; we must do" *(Johann Wolfgang von Goethe)*.

"There is no greater hell than the prison of fear" *(Ben Johnson, 1572)*.

"The way of the pioneer is always rough" *(Harvey Firestone, 1868)*.

"Bravery is the only one that knows that you are afraid" *(Franklin Jones)*.

"The strongest man in the world is he who stands alone" *(Henrik Ibsen, 1828)*.

"Falsehood is cowardice; the truth courage" *(Hosea Ballou, 1771)*.

"When you do things motivated by fear, you generally do the wrong thing" *(Gary Oliver)*.

"You realize sometimes that nobody is going to do anything about it unless you do" *(Barack Obama, 1961)*.

"No one stands so tall until he stoops to help a child" *(Abraham Lincoln, 1809)*.

"It is easier to build strong children than to repair broken men" *(Frederick Douglass, 1817).*

"When one's mind is made up, this diminishes fear; knowing what must be done does away with fear" *(Rosa Parks, 1913).*

OMEGA

"AVOIDING A FIGHT IS A MARK OF HONOR,
ONLY A FOOL INSISTS ON QUARRELING"
(PROV. 20:03).

thinking ...judging ...
understanding ...
learning ...

ALPHA

"MY CHILD DON'T LOSE SIGHT OF
COMMON SENSE AND DISCERNMENT,
HOLD ON TO THEM"
(PROV. 3:21).

"No legacy is so rich as honesty" *(William Shakespeare, 1564).*

"Once you make a decision, the universe conspires to make it happen" *(Ralph Waldo Emerson, 1803).*

"If you would hit the mark, you must aim a little above it" *(Henry Wadsworth Longfellow, 1807).*

"Be curious not judgmental" *(Walt Whitman, 1819).*

"The more unjust you anger, the more likely that you will regret it later."

"There is no arguing with the inevitable. The only argument available with the east wind is to put on an overcoat" *(James Russell Lowell, 1819).*

"Believe you can and you're halfway there" *(Theodore Roosevelt, 1859).*

"Difficulties mastered are opportunities won."

"It's a fine thing to be honest, but it is also very important to be right."

"It is a mistake to look too far ahead. Only one link in the chain of destiny can be handled at a time."

"Let our advanced worrying become our advanced thinking and planning."

"Out of intense complexities, intense simplicities emerge."

"The empires of the future are the empires of the mind."

"To improve is to change. To be perfect is to change often."

"To build may have to be slow and laborious tasks of years.

To destroy can be the thoughtless act of a simple day" *(Winston Churchill, 1874).*

"Once harm has been done even a fool understands it" *(Homer, 800 BC).*

"The art of leadership is saying no, not yes. It is very easy to say yes" *(Tony Blair).*

"Oh be very sure that no man will learn anything at all unless he first will learn humility."

"Refuse to be ill, never tell people you are ill; never own it to yourself."

"The pen is mightier than the sword."

"Anger ventilated often hurries toward forgiveness; anger concealed often hardens into revenge" *(Robert Bulwer Lytton, 1803).*

"You aren't learning anything when you are talking" *(Lyndon B. Johnson 1908).*

"You will never be sorry for thinking before acting."

"It's always in season for old men to learn" *(Aeschylus, 525 BC).*

"Focus on your goals. Live during the journey" *(E.A.F.).*

"Mistakes are made to be corrected, not repeated" *(Lavoy Frazier).*

"Suffering is another name for the teaching of experience, which is the parent of instruction, and the school master of life."

"Cease to inquire what the future has in store and take as a gift whatever the day brings forth."

"In adversity always keep an even mind."

"If you think you're weak poor, you'll think you're weak rich. Money is not the answer."

"Service to others is the rent you pay for your room here on earth" *(Shirley Chisholm).*

"There are some bridges that need to be burned, so that you don't cross them again"*(E.A.F.).*

"Slight not what's near through aiming at what is far."

"This is slavery, not to speak one's thoughts."

"There is just one life for each of us; our own" *(Euripides, 480 BC).*

"Civil Rights comparison: I've met a lot of former homosexuals, but never a former African American."

"When in doubt, under promise and over deliver."

"Quick decisions are unsafe decisions" *(Sophocles, 496 BC).*

"Know how to listen and you will profit even from someone who talks badly."

"Let not your mind run on what you lack as much as on what you have already" *(Plutarch, 46 AD)*.

"Don't think that you always have to be cheerful and positive; grief and depression take time to heal."

"Say not always what you know, but always know what you say" *(Claudius, 10 BC)*.

"Who thinks most, feels noblest, acts the best" *(Philip James Bailey)*.

"It's not what people call you, it's what you answer to."

"Powerful indeed is the empire of habit."

"The eyes are not responsible when the mind does the seeing" *(Publius Syrus, 85 BC)*.

"You cannot parcel out freedom in pieces because freedom is all or nothing" *(Tertullian, 160 BC)*.

"When giving advice be sure, and if you love someone don't tell them anything wrong" *(Margie Hardnett)*.

"It is better to be not known, than to be known for the wrong reasons."

"There is a difference between being noted and being notorious; there is a difference between being famous and being infamous" *(Otonya Allen)*.

"There is nothing so satisfying to the spirit, so defining of your character, than giving your all to a difficult task" *(Barack Obama, 1961)*.

"If everyone is thinking alike somebody is not thinking."

"Your choice chooses your consequences" *(Ed Young).*

"It is well for one to know more than he says."

"Things we do not expect happen more frequently than we wish" *(Titus Maccius Plautus, 254 BC).*

"It's not what you think, it's how you think."

"A learned man always has riches in himself" *(Phaedrus, 15 BC).*

"Where our senses fail us, reason must step in" *(Galileo Galilei, 1564).*

"When I write something, every word of it is meant. I can't say it enough" *(Anne Rice, 1941).*

"Jests that cause pain are no jests" *(Migel de Cervantes, 1547).*

"Stop worrying. Accept your limitations. Have faith in people. Spend some time alone. Try to want what you have, instead of spending your strength trying to get what you want"*(Abraham L Feinberg).*

"All that we are not stares back at what we are."

"Learn from your dreams what you lack" *(W. H. Auden, 1907).*

"Do not read, as children do, to amuse yourself, or like the ambitious, for purpose and instruction; no read in order to live" *(Gustave Flaubert, 1821).*

"You don't notice change in what is always before you" *(Honore de Balzac)*.

"None know the weight of another's burden" *(George Herbert, 1593)*.

"Books are like imprisoned souls until someone takes them off the shelf and frees them" *(Samuel Butler, 1835)*.

"If we understand the past, we are most likely to understand what is happening around us" *(Helen Dunmore 1952)*.

"Unreasonable haste is the direct road to error" *(Moliere, 1622)*.

"The ear of the leader must ring with the voices of the people" *(Woodrow Wilson, 1856)*.

"Learn to listen; it's as simple as that" *(Antonio Johnson)*.

"Eat the meat and leave the bone. Take what you need from every experience and leave what you don't need" *(Jennifer Jenkins)*.

"The reward of suffering is experience" *(Harry Truman, 1884)*.

"Failure is a few errors in judgment repeated everyday."

"If you go to work on your goals, your goals will go to work on you. If you go to work on your plan, your plan will go to work on you. Whatever good things we build end up building us" *(Jim Rohn, 1930)*.

"You don't have to look for trouble, it will find you."

"Never make decisions based on emotions."

"A degree is like a flag that you can wave throughout your life" *(E.A.F).*

ALPHA OMEGA

"Interfering in someone else's
conversation is as foolish
as yanking a dogs ear"
(Prov. 26:17).

"When arguing with your neighbor,
don't betray another person's secret,
others will accuse you of gossip,
and you will never regain
your good reputation"
(Prov. 25:9).

"Whatsoever a man thinks,
that's what he is."
(Prov. 23:7).

"Trust is something to be earned."

"Poverty is a disease of the mind."

"Your body is listening to whatever you tell it; watch what you say to it."

"It is a mark of an educated mind to be able to entertain a thought without accepting it."

"It's called a pen, it's like a printer, hooked straight to the brain."

"Obstacles are those frightful things you see when you take your eyes off your goals" *(Henry Ford, 1863)*.

"Nearly all men can stand adversity, but if you want to test character give him power" *(Abraham Lincoln, 1809)*.

"As long as you are going to be thinking anyway, think big" *(Donald Trump)*.

"If you don't understand something, don't do anything, it is time to wait."

"A man that goes alone can start today, but he that travels with another has to wait for him" *(Henry David Thoreau, 1817)*.

"A man can't ride your back unless you're bent" *(M.L.K, 1929)*.

ALPHA OMEGA
"AVOID ALL PERVERSE TALK,
STAY AWAY FROM CORRUPT SPEECH"
(PROV. 4:24).

"SPOUTING OFF WITHOUT LISTENING TO THE FACTS IS BOTH SHAMEFUL AND FOOLISH"

(Prov. 18:13).

"Learn as much by writing as by reading" *(Lord Acton, 1834).*

"You are the sum total of your thoughts."

"It is better to be a 'has been' than a 'never was'" *(Northcote Parkinson).*

"There are some events and occurrences that should not be shared" *(Teresa Hairston).*

"Conflict cannot survive without participation."

"When you judge another, you do not define them; you define yourself" *(Wayne Dyer).*

"It's not unseemly for a man to die fighting in defense of his country" *(Homer, 800 BC).*

"No bridge was ever built by good intentions"

"If I am what I have and I lose what I have, who am I?" *(Erich Fromm).*

"It is better to sleep on a thing beforehand than to lie awake about them afterwards."

"Know to listen to those who know" *(Baltasar Gracian, 1601).*

"Much learning does not teach understanding" *(Herodotus, 484 BC).*

"Cursing, drinking and smoking do not make you a grown-up."

"When you have to make a choice and don't make it, it is indeed a choice" *(William James)*.

"Hope never abandons you; you abandon it" *(George Weinberg)*.

"We are twice armed when we fight with faith" *(Plato, 427 BC)*.

"Talent is on loan from God" *(Rush)*.

"Don't argue too long with a fool, because the listeners won't be able to tell the difference."

"Unless we place our religion and treasure in the same thing, religion will always be sacrificed" *(Epictelus, 55)*.

"Charm is a way of getting the answer 'yes' without asking a clear question."

"Integrity has no need for rules."

"Stupidity has a knack of getting its way" *(Albert Camus)*.

"The future starts today not tomorrow" *(Pope John Paul II, 1920)*.

"There are only so many tomorrows."

"Everyone who got where he is, had to begin where he was" *(Pope John Paul VI, 1897)*.

"The only way to make a man trustworthy is to trust him" *(Henry Stimson)*.

"No problem can ever be solved from the same level of consciousness that created it. Once we accept our limits, we go beyond them" *(Albert Einstein 1879)*.

"If passion drives you, let reason hold the reins" *(Benjamin Franklin, 1706)*.

ALPHA OMEGA

"A FALSE WITNESS WILL NOT GO
UNPUNISHED NOR WILL A LIAR ESCAPE"
(PROV. 19:5).

"THOSE WHO STRAY AWAY
FROM COMMON SENSE WILL END UP
IN THE COMPANY OF THE DEAD"
(PROV. 21:16).

"The key to failure is trying to please everybody" *(Bill Cosby)*.

"If you search for the good, you will find it."

"Honest error is to be pitied not ridiculed" *(Lord Chesterfield, 1694)*.

"I would rather appreciate things I cannot have than have things that I cannot appreciate."

"Secrets are things we give to others to keep for us" *(Elbert Hubbard)*.

"Every adversity, every failure, every headache carries with it the seed of an equal or greater benefit."

"If you cannot do great things, do small things in a great way."

"Most great people have attained their greatest success just one step beyond their greatest failure."

"Nature cannot be tricked or cheated. She will give up to you the object of your struggle only after you have paid her price."

"When defeat comes, accept it as a signal that your plans are not sound; rebuild those plans and set sail once again toward your coveted goal" *(Napoleon Hill).*

"Be able to defend your argument in a rational way; otherwise, all you have is an opinion."

"Understand why casinos and racetracks stay in business—the gambler always loses over the long term" *(Marilyn vos Savant).*

"Learn to get in touch with the silence within yourself, and know that everything in life has purpose" *(Elisabeth Kubler).*

"The only person that is educated is the one who has learned how to learn, and change" *(Carl Rogers).*

"The problem is not that there is a problem. The problem is expecting otherwise and thinking having a problem is a problem" *(Theodore Isaac Rubin).*

"The stupid neither forgive nor forget; the naive forgives and forgets; the wise forgives but do not forget" *(Thomas Szasz).*

"Conviction is worthless unless converted into conduct."

"The greatest of all faults, is to be conscious of none" *(Thomas Carlyle).*

"It doesn't matter if the water is cold or warm if you're going to have to wade through it anyway" *(Teilhard de Chardin).*

"Books are the quietest friends, most accessible and wisest counselors, and most patient teachers" *(Charles W. Eliot).*

"All causes are essentially mental, and whosoever comes into daily contact with a high order of thinking must take on some of it" *(Charles Fillmore, 1854).*

"Washing your hands of the conflict between the powerful and powerless is to side with the powerful" *(Paulo Freire, 1921).*

"There is one word in America that says it all, and that one word is 'you never know'" *(Joaquin Andujar).*

"The road to the sacred leads through the secular" *(Abraham Joshua Herschel, 1907).*

"It is well to think well. It is divine to act well" *(Horace Mann, 1796).*

"The essence of strategy is choosing what not to do" *(Michael Porter, 1909).*

"It is wrong always, everywhere, and for anyone, to believe anything, upon insufficient evidence."

"No man can hold another man down in the ditch without remaining down in the ditch with him.

You must reinforce arguments with results" *(Booker T. Washington).*

"In order to win, you must expect to win" *(Richard Bach, 1936).*

"The way that you empower yourself is read."

"An encounter with God is an unexpected expectation."

"Your thinking will be transformed by the conflicts in your life."

"Anytime there is a war, there is something that is put to death, that your thinking might change."

"Your abilities are defined or refined by facing opposition or conflict."

"Something that appears to be hard is really easy; you just need someone to show you."

"You can never learn less, you can only learn more."

"Common sense is that which judges things given to it by the other senses."

"Experience does not err; only our judgment errs, by

expecting from her other than what is not in her power" *(Leonardo da Vinci, 1452)*.

"A man is not idle because he is absorbed in thought. There is a visible labor and there is an invisible labor" *(Victor Hugo, 1802)*.

"It does not matter which side of the fence you get off on sometimes. What matters most is getting off. You cannot make progress without making decisions.

The major reason for setting goals is for what it makes of you to accomplish it. What it makes of you will always be the greater value than what you get.

Time is more valuable than money. You can get more money, but you can't get more time.

Without a sense of urgency, desire loses its value *(Jim Rohn, 1930)*.

"The best vision is insight."

"Thinking well is wise, planning well, wiser; doing well wisest of all."

"When you cease to dream, you cease to live" *(Malcolm Forbes, 1917)*.

"There is only one sort of discipline, perfect discipline" *(George Patton, 1885)*.

"It is a terrible thing to see and have no vision."

"No pessimist ever discovered the secret of the stars, or sailed to an uncharted land, or opened a new doorway for the human spirit" *(Helen Keller, 1880)*.

"Change what you do; change what you get" *(E.J. Ford, 1998).*

"What the mind cannot retain, the body must endure" *(Edwin Louis Cole).*

"No one can possibly know what is about to happen; it is happening, each time, for the first time, for the only time."

"Not everything that is faced can be changed, but nothing can be changed until it is faced" *(James Baldwin).*

"A child cannot be taught by anyone who despises him, and a child cannot afford to be fooled" *(Gertrude Stein).*

"He that cannot forgive others, breaks the bridge over which he must pass himself; for every man has need to be forgiven" *(Thomas Fuller, 1608).*

"If there exist no possibility of failure, victory is meaningless" *(Robert Schuller).*

"Every problem has in it the seeds of its own solution. If you don't have any problems you don't get any seeds.

The person that sends out positive thoughts activates the world around him positively and draws back to himself positive results.

When every physical and mental resources is focused, ones power to solve a problem multiplies tremendously" *(Norman Vincente Peale 1898).*

"It is much easier to go downhill than up, but the view is much better from the top" *(Henry Ward Beecher).*

"Wrong is wrong no matter who does it or who says it" *(Malcolm X).*

"The future enters into us in order to transform itself in us, long before it happens."

"There are no classes in life for beginners; right away you are always asked to deal with what is most difficult" *(Rainer Maria Rilke).*

"Writing is learning to say nothing more clearly each day" *(William Allingham, 1821).*

"A hungry stomach cannot hear" *(Jean de la Fontaine, 1621).*

"No tears in the writer, no tears in the reader" *(Robert Frost, 1874).*

"Your secret is your prisoner; once you reveal it you become its slave" *(Solomon Ibn Gabirol).*

"Friendship is always a sweet responsibility, never an opportunity."

"Generosity is giving more than you can, and pride is taking less than you need" *(Kahil Gibran).*

"Only by joy and sorrow does a person know anything about themselves and their destiny. They learn who to do and what to avoid" *(Johann Wolfgang Von Goethe).*

"Weigh the meaning and look not at the words" *(Ben Johnson).*

"Ask questions, gain knowledge" *(Stephanie Harris).*

"Apprehension of that which is false is not understanding."

"Time stays long enough for who will use it" *(Leonardo da Vinci, 1452).*

"Vision, it reaches beyond the thing that is, into the conception of what can be. Imagination gives you the picture. Vision gives you the impulse to make the picture your own" *(Robert Collier).*

"There are always two solutions to any problem."

"Remember fair is a perception."

"You have been engineered to solve problems" *(I. V. Hilliard).*

"Stock and enrich your memory, a man thinks with his memory."

"Even the jailbird sings" *(Shirley Caesar).*

"They say that practice makes perfect, no, perfect practice makes perfect.

You could be doing something for thirty years and be doing it all wrong. Embrace new ideas" *(John Diggins).*

"Liberalism: 'Our programs are not working; let us continue.'"

"The secret to having a personal life is not answering too many questions about it" *(Joan Collins).*

"When an action is once done, it is right or wrong forever."

"Use sound judgments to make good decisions and live with the consequences" *(Nick Popaditch)*.

"Understand the difference between being common and being unique" *(Donnie McClurklin)*.

"Every top stands on its own bottom; make your foundation strong and get things for yourself."

"Remember even at your worst, you still have control over your anger."

"When seeking revenge, first dig two graves."

"When you think nobody is watching or sees, trust me somebody is" *(E.A.F.)*.

"It is safe to make a choice in telling your thoughts, scarcely is it safe to tell them all."

"Just because you can't find a solution does not mean there isn't one."

"The cost of liberty is less than the price of repression" *(W.E.B. Du Bois, 1868)*.

OMEGA

"IT IS BETTER TO BE PATIENT
THAN POWERFUL; BETTER TO HAVE SELF-
CONTROL THAN CONQUER A CITY"
(PROV. 16:32).

wisdom ... knowledge ...
truth ... spirituality ...

ALPHA

"ALL THINGS WERE MADE BY HIM;
AND WITHOUT HIM WAS NOT
ANYTHING MADE THAT WAS MADE"
(JOHN 1:3).

"Above all, to thine own self be true" *(William Shakespeare, 1564)*.

"If you talk to a man in a language he understands, that goes to his head. If you talk to a man in his language, it goes to his heart" *(Nelson Mandela, 1918)*.

"Don't give your feelings divine authority!"

"When God wants a great work done in the world, He puts it in a mother's heart, then she puts it in the baby's mind. The greatest forces in the world are babies" *(E. T. Sullivan)*.

"The best way out is always through" *(Robert Frost, 1874)*.

"To keep your secret is wisdom, but to expect others to keep it is folly" *(Samuel Johnson, 1709)*.

"Don't hit at all if it is honorably possible to avoid hitting. But never hit soft" *(Theodore Roosevelt, 1859)*.

"You young people, you haven't gotten to be where old people are yet, but they have been where you are; listen to your elders" *(Bobby Watkins)*.

"If you're going through hell, keep going."

"The truth is incontrovertible, malice may attack it, ignorance may deride it, but in the end, there it is."

"There is no such thing as a good tax."

"We are masters of the unsaid words, but slaves of those we let slip out."

"We shape our dwelling, afterwards our dwelling shapes us" *(Winston Churchill, 1874)*.

"Like an old leaning barn sometimes you have to ask God to prop you up, as you grow older on your leaning side."

"God loves each of us as if there were only one of us" *(St. Augustine, 354)*.

"You can't punish people for God" *(Erica Ford, 1986)*.

"No rational man can be convinced about the reality of hell and do nothing about it."
    Other people's misery should not extinguish your joy. When you're eating steak, you don't think about the starving in China" *(Robert Jeffress)*.

"The true spirit of conversation is building on another man's observation, not overturning it" *(Robert Bulwer Lytton, 1831)*.

"No man ever listened himself out of a job" *(Calvin Coolidge, 1872)*.

"Honesty is the first chapter in the book of wisdom" *(Thomas Jefferson, 1743)*.

"Do not pray for easy lives, pray for stronger men" *(John F. Kennedy, 1917)*.

"You're either born once and die twice, or born twice and die once."

"What's popular is not always right, and what is right is not always popular" *(Destini Ford, 1993)*.

"Why do you hasten to remove anything which hurts your eye, while if something affects your soul you postpone the care until next year" *(Horace, 65 BC).*

"Beauty is not caused, it is."

"You can know the price of a thing and still not know its value" *(Lord Hunt).*

"Saying nothing sometimes says the most" *(Emily Dickerson, 1830).*

"Memory is the mother of all wisdom."

"To be free from evil thoughts is God's best gift" *(Aeschylus, 525 BC).*

"At the moment of death, both rich and poor are naked and empty-handed before God."

"Begin, be bold, and venture to be wise" *(Horace, 65 BC).*

"New Year's Day is everyman's birthday" *(Charles Lamb, 1775).*

"The truth means responsibility; that's why everyone dreads it."

"Truth was never indebted to a lie" *(Edward Young, 1683).*

"God never made His work for man to mend" *(John Dryden, 1631).*

"If a person hasn't come to a point one time in his life, that he/she has shed a tear, simply because they love

God, and know how good he has been to them, simply does not really know God" *(E.A.F).*

"Faith does not demand details."

"Right is Right even if everyone is against it, and wrong is wrong even if everyone is for it" *(William Penn, 1644).*

"You must not fight too often with the same enemy, or you will teach him your art of war" *(Napoleon Bonaparte, 1769).*

"Fear and faith cannot live in the same body" *(Rod Parsely).*

"Because of consternation (dismay) many will not receive" *(Donald Lewis).*

"Nothing is beautiful from every point of view."

"One wanders to the left, another to the right. Both are equally in error, both are seduced by different delusions."

"The righteous are like carving upon stone for the smallest act is durable."

"Undeservedly, you will atone for the sins of your fathers."

"You are free to yield to the truth."

"Words will not fail when the matter is well considered" *(Horace, 65 BC).*

"Among mortals second thoughts are wisest."

"Some wisdom you must learn from one who is wise."

"Ten soldiers wisely led will beat a hundred with no head."

"Silence is wisdom's best reply" *(Euripides, 480 BC).*

"It is terrible to speak well and be wrong."

"No enemy is worse than bad advice."

"Your happiness depends on wisdom all the way."

"Trust dies, but mistrust blossoms" *(Sophocles, 496 BC).*

ALPHA OMEGA

"GOD IS NOT A MAN, SO HE DOES NOT LIE.
HE IS NOT HUMAN SO HE DOES NOT
CHANGE HIS MIND"
(PROV. 23:19).

"A fool and a liar don't think about money" *(Mike Murdock).*

"Go with God, he will go with you" *(Shaun Rabb).*

"You can't pay man for what God does."

"To do no evil is good, to intend none is better" *(Claudius, 10 BC).*

"God looks at the clean hands, not the full ones."

"He who spares the bad injures the good."

"How unhappy is he who cannot forgive himself."

"No one is exposed to danger who, even when in safety is always on their guard."

"Some remedies are worse than the disease" *(Publilius Syrus, 85 BC).*

"Nothing that is God's is attained by money."

"The first reaction to truth is hatred" *(Tertullian, 160 AD).*

"One eyewitness is better than a hundred hear-sayers" *(Titus Maccius Plautus, 254 BC).*

"Whoever is detected in a shameful fraud is ever not believed even if they speak the truth" *(Phaedrus, 15 BC).*

"A word is dead when it is said, some say. I say it just begins to live that day" *(Emily Dickinson, 1830).*

"Those things that costs less is less valued" *(Miguel de Cervantes, 1547).*

"Power is no blessing in itself, except when it is used to protect the innocent" *(Jonathan Swift, 1667).*

"Be not the first by whom the new is tried, nor the last to lay the old aside."

"Nature and nature's laws lay hid at night; God said, 'let Newton be' and all was light."

"No one should be ashamed to admit they are wrong, which is but saying, in other words, that they are wiser today than they were yesterday."

"To err is human, to forgive is divine" *(Alexander Pope, 1688).*

"The moment you pray for somebody else you cannot hate them" *(Kathie Lee Gifford).*

"It is better to understand a little than misunderstand a lot" *(Anatole France, 1844).*

"Confess your sins to the Lord and you will be forgiven; confess to man and you will be laughed at" *(Josh Billings, 1818).*

"Prayer should be the key of the day and the lock of the night."

"War makes thieves and peace hangs them" *(George Herbert, 1593).*

"All truth is not to be told at all times" *(Samuel Butler).*

"In the middle of your setback you need to be planning your comeback" *(Joel Olsteen).*

"I would rather lose in a cause that will someday win than win in a cause that will someday lose."

"The man who is swimming against the stream knows the strength of it" *(Woodrow Wilson, 1856).*

"You don't have to defend God, He can defend himself" *(E.A.F.).*

"Never give anybody hell, just tell them the truth and they will think it's hell" *(Harry Truman, 1884).*

"Charity is injurious unless it helps the recipient to become independent of it" *(John D. Rockefeller, 1839).*

"Giving is better than receiving because giving starts the receiving process."

"If you don't design your own life plan, chances are you'll fall into someone else's plan. And guess what they have planned for you? Not much" *(Jim Rohn, 1930).*

"The things that you praise God about the most are the things that you can't talk about or testify about" *(Anthony Wilcox).*

"Time heals all wounds."

"It's better to say 'there he went' than 'there he lay." *(Willie Ford)*

ALPHA OMEGA

"LIFE AND DEATH IS IN THE POWER OF THE TONGUE" (PROV. 18:21).

"SIMPLY LET YOUR YES BE YES, AND YOUR NO BE NO" (JAS.5: 12).

"IT'S THE LITTLE FOXES THAT SPOIL THE VINE" (SOL. 2:15).

"THE FEAR OF THE LORD
IS THE BEGINNING OF WISDOM"
(111:10).

"Poverty confines no man that has faith."

"Man is not in the world to set it right, but to see it rightly."

"Experience is the best teacher, but some things you don't want to experience."

"Prayer is the most powerful thing on earth."

"High achievements always take place because of high expectations" *(Charles Kettering)*.

"Failure does not mean that you are a failure; it just means you haven't succeeded yet" *(Robert Schuller)*.

"It is better to be alone than in bad company" *(George Washington, 1732)*.

"Truth and roses both have thorns" *(Henry David Thoreau)*.

"A lie cannot live: *(M.L.K, 1929)*.

ALPHA OMEGA
"LET NOT YOUR GOOD BE EVIL SPOKEN OF"
(ROM. 14:16 KGV).

"Wisdom will save you from evil people,
from those whose words are twisted"
(Prov. 2:12).

"Let someone else praise you not your
own mouth, a stranger not your own lips."
(Prov. 27:2).

"If you set a trap for others,
you will get caught in it"
(Prov. 26:27).

"The tongue can bring death or life;
those who love to talk
will reap the consequences"
(Prov.18:21).

"Wise words satisfy like a meal,
the right words bring satisfaction"
(Prov. 18:20).

"The name of the Lord is a strong
tower, the godly run in and are safe"
(Prov. 18:10).

"Doing wrong leads to disgrace, and
scandalous behavior brings contempt"
(Prov. 18:3).

"IF YOU REPAY GOOD WITH EVIL,
EVIL WILL NEVER LEAVE YOUR HOUSE"
(PROV. 17:13).

"WALK WITH THE WISE AND BECOME WISE,
ASSOCIATE WITH FOOLS AND GET IN TROUBLE"
(PROV. 13:20).

"THE WISE DON'T MAKE A SHOW
OF THEIR KNOWLEDGE, BUT THE FOOL
BROADCAST THEIR FOOLISHNESS"
(PROV. 12:23).

ALPHA OMEGA
"TRUTHFUL WORDS STAND THE TEST
OF TIME BUT A LIE IS SOON EXPOSED"
(PROV. 12:29).

"YOUR KINDNESS WILL REWARD YOU;
YOUR CRUELTY WILL DESTROY YOU"
(PROV. 11:17).

"THE BLESSING OF THE LORD MAKES A
PERSON RICH AND ADDS NO SORROW TO IT"
(PROV. 10:22).

"TOO MUCH TALK LEADS TO SIN,
BE SENSIBLE AND KEEP YOUR MOUTH SHUT"
(PROV. 10:19).

"IF YOU PRIZE WISDOM SHE WILL MAKE YOU
GREAT, EMBRACE HER SHE WILL HONOR YOU"
(PROV. 4:8).

"DO NOT TURN YOUR BACK ON WISDOM
SHE WILL PROTECT YOU"
(PROV. 4:6).

"Opinions alter, manners change, creeds rise and fall, but the moral laws are written on the tables of eternity."

"Sooner or later man has always had to decide whether he worships his own power, or the power of God" *(Lord Acton)*.

"There is no need in childhood as strong as the need for a parent's protection."

"A single lie destroys a reputation of integrity."

"Let the first impulse pass, wait for the second" *(Baltasar Gracian, 1601)*.

"No man has ever stepped in the same river twice, for it is not the same river and he is not the same man" *(Herodotus, 484)*.

"The sovereign cure for worry is prayer."

"Wisdom is knowing what to overlook" *(William James)*.

"There is no greater rudeness than to interrupt another's conversation" *(John Locke, 1632)*.

"Teach thy tongue to say 'I don't know' and thou shall progress" *(Mamonides, 1135)*.

"Kind words do not cost much, but they accomplish much" *(Blaise Paschal, 1623)*.

"It is only the dead that have seen the end of war."

"Necessity is the mother of invention."

"Wise men talk because they have something to say, a fool because they have to say something" *(Plato, 428)*.

"We have two ears and one mouth so that we can listen twice as much as we speak" *(Epictelus, 55)*.

"Good can exist without evil whereas evil cannot exist without good" *(Saint Thomas Aquinas)*.

"An excuse is worse and more terrible than a lie, for an excuse is a lie guarded."

"Stupidity is also a gift of God, but one mustn't misuse it" *(Pope J Paul II, 1920)*.

"When you walk through a storm hold your head up high and don't be afraid, walk with hope in your heart" *(Shirley Bradley)*.

"Nothing makes one feel so strong as to call for help."

"The older the fiddler the sweeter the tune" *(Pope J Paul IV)*.

"God made the country and man made the town."

"There is nothing more powerful than a concept and nothing more dangerous than a misconception" *(Myles Munroe)*.

"We came equals into this world, and equals shall we go out of it" *(George Mason)*.

"When the solution is simple, God is answering" *(Albert Einstein, 1879)*.

"When you say that a situation or person is hopeless, you slam the door in the face of God" *(Charles Allen, 1913)*.

"Keep cool, anger is not an argument" *(Daniel Webster, 1782)*.

"Knowledge gives weight but accomplishment gives luster, and many more people see than weigh" *(Lord Chesterfield)*.

"Lost time is never found again."

"Observe all men, thyself most."

"The absent is never at fault nor the present without excuse."

"The doors of wisdom are never shut."

"The man that trades freedom for security does not nor will he ever receive either."

"There was never a good war or a bad peace."

"Well done is better than well said."

"When in doubt, don't."

"Work as if you would live a hundred years. Pray as if you were to die tomorrow."

"A small leak can sink a great ship."

"An investment in knowledge pays the best interest."

"Half a truth is often a great lie."

"He that is of the opinion that money will do anything may well do anything for money."

"He that won't be counseled can't be helped."

"Hear reason or she will make you feel her."

"It is easier to prevent bad habits than to break them."

"It is only when the rich are sick do they feel the impotency of wealth" *(Benjamin Franklin, 1706)*.

ALPHA OMEGA

"Discipline your children while
there is hope otherwise
you will ruin their lives"
(Prov. 19:18).

"IF YOU STOP LISTENING TO INSTRUCTION
YOU TURN YOUR BACK ON KNOWLEDGE"
(PROV. 19:27).

"THOSE WHO SHUT THEIR EYES TO THE POOR
WILL BE IGNORED IN THEIR OWN TIME OF NEED"
(PROV. 21:13).

"STOLEN BREAD TASTES SWEET
BUT IT TURNS TO GRAVEL IN THE MOUTH"
(PROV. 20:17).

"NO HUMAN WISDOM OR UNDERSTANDING,
OR PLAN CAN STAND AGAINST GOD"
(PROV. 21:30).

"Genius has its limitation, but stupidity does not."

"The supernatural is the natural not yet understood."

"The church saves sinners; but science seeks to stop their manufacture" *(Elbert Hubbard)*.

"Be able to keep a secret or a promise when you know it is the right thing to do."

"Being defeated is often a temporary condition. Giving up is what makes it permanent."

"To acquire knowledge, one must study; but to acquire wisdom, one must observe" *(Marilyn vos Savant)*.

"The promise land always lies on the other side of the wilderness" *(Henry Ellis)*.

"Forgiveness means letting go of the past" *(Gerald Jampolsky)*.

"To shun one's cross is to make it heavier" *(Henry Frederic Amiel)*.

"We are not human beings having a spiritual experience. We are spiritual beings having a human experience" *(Pierre Teilhard de Chardin)*.

"Wars don't determine who is right—only who is left" *(Bertrand Russell, 1872)*.

"Life is finite; live as if it will come to an end because one day it will"*(E.A.F, 1964)*.

"The issue of prayer is not prayer; the issue of prayer is God" *(Abraham Joshua Hershel, 1907)*.

"Seek not greatness, but seek truth and you will find both" *(Timothy Leary, 1920)*.

"Tomorrow is always fresh with no mistakes in it" *(Lucy Maud Montgomery, 1874)*.

"Not being known does not stop the truth from being true" *(Richard Bach, 1936)*.

"God did not put you in this world to be a nobody" *(Baron Hopgood)*.

"When you start it, God will bring the increase."

"Those who play with the devil's toys will be brought by degrees to wield his sword" *(R. Buckminster Fuller, 1895)*.

"There is no greater harm than that of wasted time" *(Michelangelo, 1475)*.

"How we answer the problems and situations in life defines us" *(Joni Lamb)*.

"It is better to be hurt by the truth than to gain satisfaction from the lies" *(David Allen, 1744)*.

"For every situation there is grace. Then there is glory" *(Jack Graham)*.

"Truth exists, only lies are invented" *(George Brague, 1882)*.

"Miss a meal if you have to, but don't miss a book. The book you don't read won't help."

"Take care of your body; it's the only place you have to live."

"The more you know the less you need to say" *(Jim Rohn, 1930)*.

"Age wrinkles the body. Quitting wrinkles the soul."

"There is no security on this earth, there is only opportunity" *(Douglas MacArthur, 1880)*.

"The world is full of suffering; it is also full of the overcoming of it" *(Helen Keller, 1880)*.

"Remember life is not a sprint, it is a marathon, don't give up."

"Change is not one big choice, but a thousand little ones" *(T.D. Jakes).*

"Boundaries are to protect life not limit pleasures."

"Crying over what's gone won't find the present."

"Expectancy is the atmosphere of miracles."

"Faith is the ticket to the feast, not the feast."

"Knowledge of God's work is the bulwark against deception, temptation, accusation and even persecution" *(Edwin Lewis Cole).*

"The price one pays for pursuing any profession, or calling, is an intimate knowledge of its ugly side" *(James Baldwin, 1924).*

"It is madness for sheep to talk peace with a wolf."

"Tis better to suffer wrong than to do it" *(Thomas Fuller, 1608).*

"You someday realize that the reason you never changed before is because you didn't want to" *(Robert Schuller).*

"Say what you mean and mean what you say" *(Stanley Ford).*

"When you pray for anyone, you tend to modify your personal attitude toward them" *(Norman Vincente Peale, 1898).*

"The secret to giving advice is, after you have honestly given it, be perfectly indifferent whether it is taken or not and never persist in trying to set people right" *(Henry Ward Beecher).*

"Wear the old coat and buy the new book" *(Austin Phelps).*

"Have thy tools ready. God will find the work" *(Charles Kingley).*

"Right is its own defense."

"You don't have to pray to God anymore when there are storm clouds in the sky. But you do have to be insured" *(Bertolt Brecht).*

"Do what's right because it is right and do it right" *(Creflo Dollar).*

"Cities reveal themselves at night" *(Rupert Brooke, 1887).*

"And gain is gain, however small" *(Robert Browning, 1817).*

"The minority which is right will one day be the majority: the majority that is wrong will one day be the minority."

"Plan for this world as if you expect to live forever; plan for the hereafter as if you expect to die tomorrow" *(Solomon Ibn Gabirol, 1021).*

"If God wanted you otherwise, He would have created you otherwise" *(Johann Wolfgang von Goethe).*

"The devil is compromise."

"The pillars of truth and the pillars of freedom, they are the pillars of society" *(Henrik Ibsen, 1828).*

"At times it is folly to hasten, at other times to delay. The wise do everything in its proper time" *(Ovid, 43 BC).*

"Worrying never robs tomorrow of its sorrows; it just saps today of its strength" *(A. J. Cronin).*

"The past cannot be cured" *(Elizabeth I, 1533).*

"It doesn't matter what is covered; God will uncover" *(Ed Young).*

"There is still a lot of flesh in a saved man, watch what you subject yourself to."

"The animals with the strongest shells seldom have a backbone."

"You can hope for the best, but hope is not a strategy."

"Wisdom is brought forth from God."

"Wisdom comes for the moment; you won't know until you get there."

"Wisdom is gentle because it knows and sees the big picture, and stays calm."

"When you are tunneling through, when you hit that vein of gold, stay with the gold, don't ignore the gold.

If you don't know how things work, it is hard to employ them for your use" *(Gary Oliver).*

"When you are praying for sunshine, the farmer is praying for rain. God decides when and where."

"Your need will never move the heart of God, your faith will" *(Rod Parsley)*.

"There is no greater story than a true one."

"Start with God. First lesson in learning is to bow down to Him."

"Great things are done when men and mountains meet" *(William Blake)*.

OMEGA

"ONLY FOOLS SAY IN THEIR HEARTS,
'THERE IS NO GOD'"
(Ps 53:1).

success ... love ... life ... education ...

ALPHA

"Do not withhold good from those who deserve it, when it is in your power to help them" (Prov 3:27).

"However things may seem, no evil thing is success and no good thing is a failure."

"It takes less time to do things right than to explain why you did it wrong" *(Henry Wadsworth, 1807).*

"To know is nothing at all, to imagine is everything" *(Anatole France).*

"There is a fullness of all things, even sleep and love" *(Homer, 800 BC).*

"It is no use saying, 'we are doing our best.' You have got to succeed in doing what is necessary."

"Kites rise highest against the wind—not with it."

"Success consists of going from failure to failure without loss of enthusiasm."

"We make a living by what we get, but we make a life by what we give" *(Winston Churchill, 1874).*

"Happiness is a choice that requires effort at times."

"Be not afraid of storms, learn to sail your ship" *(Aeschylus, 525 BC).*

"Don't set low goals. Set goals high enough in life that it will take a lifetime to achieve them and you keep working" *(Ted Turner).*

"Be the smartest person that you can be" *(Peggy Wimbish).*

"The measure of success is not whether you have a tough

problem to deal with, but whether it's the same problem you had last year."

"Don't waste life by selecting an inferior purpose that has no lasting value."

"The greatest lesson in life is to know that even a fool is right sometimes."

"He who postpones the hour of living is like the rustic who waits for the river to run out before he crosses."

"It is your business when the wall next door catches fire" *(Horace 65 BC).*

"Life is short no matter how long we live."

"Avoid popularity; it has many snares and no real benefit" *(William Penn 1644).*

"It is better to fail at what will ultimately succeed, than succeed at what will ultimately fail" *(Peter Marsha, 1930).*

"Events will take their course; it is no good being angry at them; he is happiest who wisely turns them to the best account."

"He is not a lover who does not love forever."

"Joint understanding stands a better chance when they benefit both sides" *(Euripides, 480 BC).*

"You can take back what you give, but you can't take back the days you live" *(Gerald Randle, 1963).*

"It is better to have common sense without education, than education without common sense."

"Rather fail with honor than succeed with fraud."

"There is no success without hardship" *(Sophocles, 496 BC)*.

"Always be in the thick of life, threading its mazes sharing its strife yet somehow singing" *(Roselle Mercier Montgomery)*.

"Wealth consists not in having great possessions but in having few wants" *(Epictelus, 55)*.

"While we are making up our minds as to when we shall begin, the opportunity is lost" *(Quintilian)*.

"You must spend money to make money" *(Titus Maccius Plautus, 254 AD)*.

"In war there is no substitute for victory" *(Douglas MacArthur, 1880)*.

"Love is not to be purchased and affection has no price" *(St. Jerome, 347 BC)*.

"It's a thin line between love and hate."

"Success consists of getting up one more time than you fall" *(Oliver Goldsmith, 1730)*.

"It's not that I'm so smart; it's just that I stay with problems longer" *(Albert Einstein, 1880)*.

"Procrastination is the thief of time."

"Wise it is to comprehend the whole" *(Edward Young, 1683)*.

"Love is not just looking at one another; it's looking in the same direction" *(Antoine de Saint-Exupery, 1900)*.

"Laws are spider webs where big flies fly past and little ones get caught."

"Nobody loves a woman because she is beautiful or ugly, stupid or intelligent. We love because we love" *(Honore de Balzac, 1799)*.

"Don't be anxious about tomorrow, for tomorrow will be anxious for itself. Let the day's own trouble be sufficient for the day" *(Samuel Butler, 1835)*.

"The quest for riches darkens the sense of right and wrong" *(Antphanes, 408 BC)*.

"Life is a race. Don't whimper if the track is rough, and the goal is distant. One day you will reach it."

"War kills men, and men deplore the loss, but war also crushes bad principles and tyrants, and so saves societies" *(Charles Caleb Colton, 1780)*.

"You are not here to merely make a living; you are here to enrich the world, and you impoverish yourself if you forget the errand" *(Woodrow Wilson, 1856)*.

"Be great first, then offer up your politics" *(Mark Davis)*.

"To the victor belong the spoils" *(Andrew Jackson, 1767)*.

"The secret to success is to own nothing, but control everything" *(Nelson Rockefeller, 1908)*.

"If you want to succeed, you should strike out on new paths, rather than travel the worn path of accepted success."

"If your only goal is to become rich, you'll never achieve it" *(John Rockefeller, 1839)*.

"Formal education will make you a living; self-education will make you a fortune."

"If someone is going down the wrong road, he doesn't need motivation to speed him up. What he needs is education to turn him around."

"Learning is the beginning of wealth. Learning is the beginning of spirituality. Searching and learning is where the miracle process begins."

"Let others lead small lives but not you. Let others argue over small things but not you. Let others cry over small hurts, but not you. Let others leave their future in other peoples hands, but not you!" *(Jim Rohn, 1930)*.

"Better to ask for a lot and get half of it than to ask for a little and get all of it" *(Joyce Myers)*.

"Always keep money in your relationship."

"Don't stop your spouse from cooking for you; it's difficult to get them started again, even if you are not hungry, eat" *(Michael Matthews)*.

"Two is company three's a crowd, leave your friend at home."

"Don't forget to love yourself, you are beautiful."

ALPHA OMEGA

"Anyone that rebukes a mocker
will get an insult in return.
Anyone who corrects the wicked
will get hurt, so don't bother
correcting mockers,
they will only hate you"
(Prov. 9:7–8).

"Expect more good out of life than bad."

"No matter how far you run from death, when you stop, that's where it was supposed to meet you."

"Women love deep, and hate deep."

"So much of life's greatest treasures are in the graveyard" (learn everything you can from your elders before they are gone).

"If your life is in disarray, check your choices."

"It's not your salary that makes you rich; it's your spending habits" *(Charles Jaffe)*.

"The way you get things done is not to mind who gets the credit for doing them" *(Benjamin Jowett)*.

"Whenever an individual decides that success has been attained progress stops" *(Thomas Watson).*

"A well ordered life is like climbing a tower; the view half way up is better than the base, and it steadily becomes finer as the horizon expands" *(William Lynn Phelps, 1865).*

"The time is always right to do what's right" *(MLK, 1829).*

"Nobody ever told me whites were suppose to sing one kind of music and blacks another- I sang what I liked in the voice I had" *(Charley Pride).*

ALPHA OMEGA
"GIVING A GIFT CAN OPEN DOORS;
IT GIVES ACCESS TO IMPORTANT PEOPLE"
(PROV. 18:16).

"To be able to look back at one's past with satisfaction is to live twice" *(Lord Acton).*

"The life that does not go into action is a failure" *(Arnold J. Toynbee).*

"One always wonder about the road not taken" *(Warren Christopher).*

"If you are living out of a sense of obligation you are a slave" *(Wayne Dyer).*

"To equal a predecessor one must have twice their worth" *(Baltisar Gracian).*

"No man is free that is not master of himself" *(Epicte-lus, 55).*

"I would rather live life as if God exists and find out he doesn't, than to live life as if he doesn't and find out he does" *(Albert Camus).*

"The best medicine that you can get is what the body can give itself. Don't die of dehydration, lack of water, lack of proper nutrition, exercise, and oxygen; without these your body will try to kill you."

"In youth the days are short and years long, in old the years are short and days are long" *(Pope Paul VI).*

"There are two great days in a person's life—the day we are born and the day we discover why" *(William Barclay, 1907).*

"I try to be the same person that I was yesterday."

"Excellence is not an exception; it is a prevailing attitude."

"There is no secret to success; it's the result of preparation, hard work and learning from failure" *(Colin Powell).*

"A person who doubts himself is like a man who enlists in the ranks of the enemy, and bears arms against himself" *(Ambrose Pierce).*

"Whatever is begun in anger ends in shame."

"Absence sharpens love, presence strengthens it."

"Having been poor is no shame, but being ashamed of it is" *(Benjamin Franklin, 1706).*

ALPHA OMEGA

"GET ALL THE ADVICE AND INSTRUCTION
YOU CAN, SO YOU WILL BE WISE
THE REST OF YOUR LIFE"
(PROV.19:20).

"THE LORD DETEST
DOUBLE STANDARDS OF EVERY KIND"
(PROV. 20:10).

"The ladder of success is never crowded at the top."

"He has achieved success who has worked well, laughed often and loved much."

"Life in abundance comes through great love."

"Pray that success will not come any faster than you are able to endure it."

"Love we give away is the only love we keep" *(Elbert Hubbard).*

"Be in the habit of getting up bright and early on the weekend. Why waste such precious time in bed?" *(Marilyn vos Savant).*

"Realizing what you really want stops you from chasing butterflies and puts you to work digging gold" *(William Moulton Marston).*

"Keep in mind that neither success, nor failure is final" *(Roger Babson).*

"Life is short; it's up to you to make it sweet" *(Sarah Louise Delany)*.

"Struggle associates with success."

"Where there is no conflict there is no conquest."

"You must believe beyond your beliefs (religion, opinions, convictions, creeds)" *(Baron Hopgood)*.

"Make measurable progress in reasonable time."

"Success is the natural consequence of consistently applying the basic fundamentals."

"Practice your communication skills so that when a important occasion arise, you will have the gift, the style, the sharpness, the clarity and emotion to move and affect other people" *(Jim Rohn, 1930)*.

"Failure is success if you learn from it."

"The biggest mistake you can make is not trying to make a living at what you enjoy most" *(Malcolm Forbes, 1917)*.

"Playing it safe is probably the most unsafe thing in the world.
You cannot stand still, you must go forward."

"Success is the sum total of small efforts repeated day in and day out."

"Your chances of success in any undertaking can always be measured by the belief in yourself" *(Robert Collier)*.

"Everything you need for a better future and success has

already been written, and guess what? All you have to do is go to the library."

"Life is short, be swift to love. Make haste to be kind" *(Henri Fredriic Amiel).*

"The education of a man is never completed until he dies" *(Robert E. Lee, 1807).*

"Life is either a great adventure or nothing" *(Helen Keller).*

"Love does not begin and end the way we think it does. Love is a battle, love is a war, and love is a growing up" *(James Baldwin).*

"Four things for success: work and pray, think and believe" *(Norman Vincente Peale, 1898).*

"Love recognizes no barriers. It jumps hurdles, leaps fences, and penetrates walls to arrive at its destination full of hope."

"All great achievement requires time" *(Maya Angelou).*

"True success is not just doing the best; it's about being the best" *(Otonya Allen).*

"Mistakes are a fact of life; it is the response to error that counts" *(Niki Giovanni, 1926).*

"You can believe in a love that asks for nothing."

"Success seems to be connected with action. Successful people keep moving. They make mistakes but they don't give up" *(Conrad Hilton, 1887).*

"Love does not dominate; it cultivates."

"Don't let a great education become a great indoctrination."

"A refusal to correct is a refusal to love."

"Relationships get sick, and if you don't work on them they will die. If it's sick whatever it is, if it is sick long enough, it will die" *(Sherman C.G. Allen).*

"The opposite of love is indifference or I don't care what happens anymore."

"If you don't decide to win in life, then what? *(Bridgett Hilliard).*

"Nothing brings more happiness in life than to serve a cause that is greater than yourself" *(John McCain).*

"Ignorance of ignorance is the death of knowledge."

"Youth is the time for the adventures of the body, but age for the triumphs of the mind" *(Logan Pearsall Smith).*

"No one who achieves success does so without the acknowledgement of others."

"The poor man is not he who is not without a cent, but he who is without a dream" *(Harry Kemp).*

"Don't be a teacher, be an awakener" *(Robert Frost, 1874).*

OMEGA

"AN INHERITANCE OBTAINED TOO EARLY
IN LIFE IS NOT A BLESSING IN THE END"
(PROV. 20:21).

sports ... women ...
marriage ... funny ...

SPORTS

ALPHA

"The only way to prove that you are a good sport is to lose" *(Ernie Banks)*.

"Everyone has limits; you just have to learn what your own limits are and deal with them accordingly" *(Nolan Ryan)*.

"When handling the ball, always look for daylight wherever daylight is" *(Julius Erving)*.

"One of the things my parents taught me was never listen to other peoples' expectations" *(Tiger Woods)*.

"Concentrate, play your game, and don't be afraid to win" *(Amy Alcott, 1956)*.

"Always keep your composure. You can't score from the penalty box; and to win you have to score" *(Horace, 65 BC)*.

"The game is like watching a movie unfold before your eyes; you only get one take" *(Kobe Bryant)*.

"I don't want them to forget Babe Ruth. I just want them to remember me" *(Hank Aaron, 1934)*.

"Winning is about heart, not just legs; its got to be in the right place" *(Lance Armstrong)*.

"Baseball is ninety percent mental and ten percent physical."

"In theory there is no difference between theory and practice, in practice there is" *(Yogi Berra, 1925)*.

"Pain is temporary. Quitting is forever" *(Lance Armstrong)*.

"I was reminded that when we lose and I strike out, a billion people in China don't care" *(Reggie Jackson)*.

"Don't let the fear of striking out hold you back.
    You just can't beat a person that never gives up" *(Babe Ruth, 1895)*.

"Talent wins games, but teamwork and intelligence wins championships" *(Michael Jordan)*.

"It doesn't matter who scores the points; it's who gets the ball to the scorer" *(Larry Bird)*.

"The only thing you can do is take and learn experience from it, positive and negative, and apply it to the future" *(Tiger Woods)*.

"Try your best, give it your all, everything you have, and don't give up" *(Magic Johnson)*.

"You can't be afraid of failure because that's the only way you can succeed" *(Lebron James)*.

"I run on the road long before I dance in the light."
    "It's not the mountain ahead to climb that wears you out; it's the pebble in your shoe."
    "Love is a net that catches hearts like fish."
    What keep me going are goals" *(Muhammad Ali)*.

WOMEN

ALPHA OMEGA

"A WISE WOMAN BUILDS HER HOME,
BUT A FOOLISH WOMAN TEARS IT DOWN
WITH HER OWN HANDS"
(PROV. 14:1).

"Women who seek to be equal with men lack ambition" *(Timothy Learey, 1920).*

"It is better to die on your feet than to live on your knees."

"You teach people how to treat you" *(Oprah Winfrey).*

"A man will do what's in the wife's eye" *(Marva).*

"A woman whose behavior indicates that she will make a scene if she is told the truth, asks to be deceived" *(Elizabeth Jenkins).*

"Never trust a husband too far or bachelor too near" *(Helen Rowland).*

"Single mothers, remember that your sons are still trying to connect internally with the father who is not there."

"When you get ready to leave, make sure that you have a made up mind" *(Peggy Wimbish).*

"Everything that you go through is an opportunity for growth."

"No matter what happens to you it does not define who you are."

"It ain't about being tired; it's about being strong."

"Women, don't be too quick to share anything; you are a precious and giving people."

"You are not born a woman; you become one" *(Simone de Beauvoir)*.

"You don't luck into things as much as you'd like to think you do. You build step by step, whether it's friendships or relationships or opportunity" *(Barbara Bush)*.

"Men are not the enemy, but fellow victims. The real enemy is women's denigration of themselves" *(Betty Friedan, 1921)*.

"You become the star when you learn how to listen" *(Oprah Winfrey)*.

"Be able to decline a date so gracefully that the person isn't embarrassed that he asked" (Marilyn vos Savant).

ALPHA OMEGA

"A BEAUTIFUL WOMAN WHO LACKS DISCRETION
IS LIKE A GOLD RING IN A PIG'S SNOUT"
(PROV. 11:22).

MARRIAGE

ALPHA OMEGA

"LET YOUR WIFE BE A FOUNDATION
OF BLESSING FOR YOU"
(PROV. 5:18).

"Don't trick your mind into thinking the love is still there if it's not. Even if it's one sided, it's still not there" *(E.A.F.)*.

"Almost no one is foolish enough to imagine automatic success in any activity. Yet almost everyone believes he automatically deserves success in marriage" *(Sydney Harris)*.

"Play together, the couples that spend all their time looking for pleasure will get tired and won't find it."

"The greatest gift that a man or woman can give to one another is their innocence, because you can only give it once."

"The bonds of matrimony are like any other bonds—they mature slowly" *(Peter De Uries)*.

"Even when you don't feel like you're in love, your friendship should keep you together" *(Sherman C.G. Allen)*.

"Getting divorced because you don't love a person is almost as silly as getting married because you do" *(Zsa Zsa Gabor)*.

"Don't fight! Have moments of intense fellowship" *(Gary Oliver)*.

"Marriage is a covenant with God. God does not break covenant, unless it is by his authority and will to release you, and not your feelings. Take marriage very seriously, you may get divorced by man but still be married by God."

"When you marry, you exchange that attention of many for the attention of one."

"A man wins nothing better than a good wife, and then again nothing worse than a bad one" *(Hesiod)*.

"Before marriage a man will be awake thinking about what you've said. After marriage he'll fall asleep before you are finished."

"A successful marriage requires falling in love many times, always with the same person" *(Mignon McLaughlin)*.

"Well married, a person has wings, poorly married shackles" *(Henry Ward Beecher)*.

"Only choose in marriage a man whom you would choose as a friend if he was a woman" *(Joseph Joubert)*.

ALPHA OMEGA

"A WORTHY WIFE IS A CROWN FOR HER HUSBAND BUT A DISGRACEFUL WOMAN IS LIKE A CANCER IN HIS BONES" (PROV. 12:4).

FUNNY

ALPHA OMEGA

"A BOWL OF VEGETABLE WITH SOMEONE
YOU LOVE IS BETTER THAN STEAK
WITH SOMEONE YOU HATE"
(PROV. 15:17).

"America is like an eagle; it takes a left wing and a right wing to fly" *(Janin Turner).*

"When I die, I want to have two funerals: for my enemies I want to be viewed with my face down—my friends, face up" *(Sherman C.G. Allen).*

"He that judges by the inches and ignores the miles should be kicked by the foot."

"The graveyard is full of people who thought they could get to heaven on the buddy pass."

"If a dog will not come to you after having looked you in the face, you should go home and examine your conscience" *(Woodrow Wilson, 1856).*

"The customers aren't always right, but they're never wrong, so what are they, confused" *(Erica Ford)?*

"Be really quick, no matter how long it takes" *(Tyler Perry).*

"We are all here on earth to help others. What on earth the others are here for, I don't know" *(W.H. Auden, 1907).*

"The only way to be sure to catch a train is to miss the one before it" *(Gilbert K. Chesterson, 1874)*.

"Don't try. Do or don't. To try is constipation."

"If you ever dream of beating me, you'd better wake up and apologize" *(Muhammad Ali)*.

"Guests are like fish, they begin to smell after a few days" *(Benjamin Franklin, 1706)*.

"When I feel like exercising, I just lie down until that feeling goes away" *(Robert M. Hutchins, 1899)*.

ALPHA OMEGA

"LAZY PEOPLE WILL TAKE THE FOOD
IN THEIR HAND BUT DON'T EVEN LIFT
TO THEIR MOUTH"
(PROV. 19:24).

CONCLUSION

"If you would not be forgotten as soon as you are dead, either write something worth reading, or do something worth writing." *(Benjamin Franklin 1706)*

Thank You,
EAF

ALPHA OMEGA

"The fear of the Lord is
the beginning of wisdom"
(Ps. 111:10).

"Through wisdom is an house builded;
and by understanding is it established:
And knowledge shall the chambers
be filled with all precious and
pleasant riches"
(Prov. 24:4 kgv).